MILESTONES OF THOUGHT

COTTON MATHER

MAGNALIA CHRISTI AMERICANA

or

The Ecclesiastical History of New England

Edited and abridged by

RAYMOND J. CUNNINGHAM

Fordham University

FREDERICK UNGAR PUBLISHING CO.
NEW YORK

MILESTONES
OF THOUGHT
in the History of Ideas

INTRODUCTION

The reappraisal of the role of Puritanism in American history and culture during the last forty years is widely acknowledged as one of the outstanding developments in modern historiography. Nineteenth century scholars and their successors early in this century, basking in the sun of rationalism, democracy, and progress, had never been entirely comfortable with the theocratic founders of New England and their seventeenth century progeny. By the late 1630's, declared Charles Francis Adams in 1893, "a theological glacier then slowly settled down upon Massachusetts, a glacier lasting through a period of nearly one hundred and fifty years, the single redeeming feature in which was that beneath the chilling and killing superincumbent mass of theology, superstition and intolerance ran the strong, vivifying current of political opposition and life." Sympathy — if not understanding — was reserved for such rebels as Roger Williams and Anne Hutchinson. At the end of the 1920's, however, Vernon L. Parrington was probably the last historian of note who could dismiss American Puritanism as "the stunted offspring of a petty environment. . . . Not a single notable book appeared; scarcely a single generous figure emerged from the primitive background."

The two scholars who principally ushered in the great reversal were Samuel Eliot Morison in his biographical studies and examination of New England's intellectual life and Perry Miller whose weighty volumes on the New England Mind completely altered our understanding of Puritan thought. Consequent upon the work of these pioneers, a host of historians have rushed to the task of restoring the reputation of the Puritans and their heritage.

Despite this revisionism, however, one man has, for the

most part, defied rehabilitation — Cotton Mather. To be
sure, various historians have acknowledged his sundry
achievements as, for example, in the field of medicine and
in his scientific observations. Morison has gone so far as to
call him "the universal genius of New England at the close
of the seventeenth century." Yet, in general, such admiration has been grudging, and the man himself has remained
an unappealing enigma. Though most of his strictures on
Puritanism have been repudiated, Parrington's assessment
of Cotton Mather remains dominant: "Intensely emotional,
high-strung and nervous, he was oversexed and over-
wrought, subject to ecstatic exaltations and, especially during his celibate years, given to seeing visions." While this is
not the place to linger over the psychological problems
posed by this complex man, a brief view of his busy life is
in order.

Scion of a famous ministerial family, Cotton Mather, who
was born in Boston on February 12, 1663, was the eldest son
of Increase Mather and the grandson of Richard Mather
and John Cotton. His early education was received at home
and at the Boston Latin School, after which, at the age of
twelve, he became the youngest student admitted to Harvard. He took his bachelor's degree in 1678 and, three
years later, his master's. Ordained to the ministry in 1685,
he served with his father until the latter's death in 1723. By
1690 Mather's capacities as preacher and author, together
with his leading role in the overthrow of Sir Edmund
Andros, the unpopular royal governor, made him one of
New England's most famous clergymen.

Never a retiring figure, Mather was zealous in behalf of
the New England Way, and he plunged enthusiastically
into political and religious controversy. He became a cham-
pión of the royal charter of 1692 and of Massachusetts' new
governor, Sir William Phips, one of his converts. It was
under Phips' auspices that the notorious witchcraft trials
were held in 1692 and 1693. Mather's role in this unfortu-
nate affair has been the subject of much debate. In his own

time, he was accused by some of his enemies of being largely responsible for the hysteria. The evidence, however, does not support this charge, and, although like most of his contemporaries he believed in the reality of witches and published several works on the subject, Mather's efforts were chiefly directed toward moderating a popular obsession which was clearly getting out of control.

While dedicated to the preservation of religious orthodoxy, Cotton Mather was not an obscurantist. Since his student days at Harvard, Mather had been interested in scientific questions, and in 1713 he was elected to the Royal Society. Similarly, in his youth he had studied medicine, and when Boston experienced a smallpox epidemic in 1721, Mather defied popular and clerical opinion by defending the use of inoculation. The same year, his publication of *The Christian Philosopher* presented doctrines that would soon become standard among American deists. Without ever abandoning the Calvinist-Congregational tradition, his practical toleration of other denominations grew with the years.

Cotton Mather's private and public life was filled with many trials. Twice a widower, he had to bear with the mental derangement of his third wife; of his fifteen children, only two survived him. Like his father, with whom he was always closely identified and whom he outlived by only five years, Mather was forced to the realization that the political, social, and economic realities of New England life at the turn of the century were at odds with the original Puritan vision. His faith was strengthened, however, by a millennial belief in the imminent Second Coming of Christ, which, shortly before his death in 1728, he proclaimed "the next thing that is to be look'd for."

But it is to Cotton Mather as a literary figure that we must direct our attention, and here we approach an area rich in significance for the student of early American intellectual life. Of all Great Britain's colonies those of New England were the most bookish. The Puritan divines were admired almost as much for their scholarship as for their piety, and one of the chief purposes for which Harvard College (whose history Mather delighted to relate) was founded was to train a learned ministry. Modeled on Cambridge University, where many early Puritans had been educated, the Harvard curriculum stressed the traditional liberal arts, amplified by a growing interest in the new science, and crowned by the study of divinity. Mather was perhaps its most brilliant product. In the course of a career devoted to a multitude of cares, he published 450 works in a wide range of literay genres: theological and devotional treatises; verse and fables; biography and history.

The seventeenth century intellectual background emphasized the study of history, which came to vie with poetry in literary esteem. To the Puritans, particularly those who emigrated to the New World, however, history was more than a cultural vogue. Interpreting their effort to establish a Holy Commonwealth within the ancient Augustinian framework of salvation history, they envisioned their task as a milestone in the unfolding of God's providential plan which, having begun with the Creation, would terminate with Christ's Last Judgment. It was their historic mission to fulfill the promise of the Reformation and to found "a City upon a Hill" which would be a light to all Christendom. Thus the American Puritans were enormously self-conscious about their sense of history, and it is not surprising that the New England colonies produced more historical prose in the seventeenth century than did any other area of English colonization. Cotton Mather's *Magnalia Christi Americana* has rightly been regarded as the climax of this trend, and an examination of this monumental work reveals the principal features of Puritan historiography.

Writing in his diary in July 1693, Mather himself provided an insight into the purpose with which he undertook his history. "And because I foresaw an inexpressible deal, of service, like to bee thereby done for the Church of God, not only here, but abroad in Europe, especially at the approaching Reformation," he recorded, "I formed a design to endeavour, the church-history of this countrey." Mather began his project later in 1693 and persevered at it amid a multitude of other cares and duties: "it hath all been done by snatches," he admitted upon its completion four years later. Still obstacles intervened, and it was not until 1702 that the *Magnalia* was finally published in London.

Although he was aware of the limitations of his work, Mather regarded it as his most important literary venture and was content to be judged by posterity on the basis of it. As to its character, the comment of Morison is just: "Almost anything you can say about the *Magnalia* will be true, in part; for it has a bit of everything, in matter, style, and method."

The first impression of Mather's church history is the looseness of its construction. Composed during precious leisure hours, the work often seems more a compilation of historical data than a coherent history. "A General Introduction" sets the tone and describes the contents of the seven books which comprise the *Magnalia,* about one-half of which is biographical in nature. In concentrating upon the lives of eminent New Englanders, clerical and lay, Mather was both perpetuating a historiographical tradition and serving the principal aim of his writing. The biographical sections are very much in the tradition of medieval hagiography, updated and Protestantized in such works as Foxe's *Book of Martyrs* (1563). Like his predecessors, Mather's aim was to praise godly men and to provide models of spirituality. This accounts for the rather stereotyped portraits which stress the religious lives of the subjects, especially noteworthy conversions and preeminent virtues. Yet, owing to advances made in biographical art during the century, with which Mather seems to have been acquainted, his lives sometimes attempt to reveal aspects of personality. His treatment of William Phips is considered one of his most successful efforts in this respect.

In judging the *Magnalia* it must be borne in mind that

Mather had little time for original research. Much of his history is composed of redactions of his own earlier work or that of others, and in the process alterations appeared which must be attributed to carelessness, craft, or art. Precision in chronology and dating is not a strong point of the history. More important — particularly in view of his insistence upon veracity — Mather did not hesitate to trim the facts to suit his purpose. Especially notorious are the strained exculpation of his grandfather, John Cotton, in the antinomian controversy and the highly idealized portrayal of the character and career of Governor Phips. Mather's consciousness of literary art, more developed than that of the earlier historians on whom he drew, is also a factor. Although he often praised simplicity and was capable of taut narrative prose, as many of the passages on Indian warfare indicate, his writing in general tended to be prolix and laden with learned allusions that reveal little more than a taste for the classics.

The *Magnalia*, however, is more than the sum of its individual parts. It is, to use the term made famous by Perry Miller, the most sustained "jeremiad" produced in seventeenth century New England. As decade passed into decade, and the religious zeal of the founders gave way to what one minister called "a dry, cold, dead frame of spirit," the clergy increasingly harried their congregations with sermons on the decadence of the day and the often all too tangible judgments of God thereby brought upon His People. They called for reformation in spirit and in deed and predicted still greater chastisements if renewal was not forthcoming. Such exhortations were frequently accompanied by appeals to the example of illustrious ancestors. By the end of the century, some clerics were prophesying the ultimate Judgment and return of Christ.

Although the jeremiads tended to become predictable and the degeneracy of which they complained greatly exaggerated by more secular standards, there is no reason to doubt their sincerity. In a half-century of extensive sociopolitical change which carried New England ever farther from the hopes of its founders, the jeremiad was the most plausible literary vehicle for bewailing a lost innocence and relieving a sense of guilt about the present and future.

Mather's great work exhibits all the characteristics of the jeremiad: idealization of the fathers; the failings of the people attended by the inevitable punishments; and finally the impending ultimate Judgment. Within the tradition of the jeremiad, Mather attempted to capture the experience of a Chosen People, with all their trials and tribulations, infusing them once again with a sense of identity and mission. For despite all evidence to the contrary, Mather did believe in the "approaching Reformation" of Christendom which by now was linked to his millennial expectations. The author of the *Magnalia* was prepared to consider whether the "errand into the wilderness" and the establishment of the New England Way, having provided a model "which He would have His churches elsewhere aspire and arise unto," "the plantation may not, soon after this, come to nothing." But this melancholy notion was perhaps too stark for one who was, after all, an American provincial, and Mather never assented to it. More congenial was the ecstatic vision he depicted in a sermon several years later: "There are many arguments to perswade us, that our glorious Lord, will have an Holy City in America. . . . We cannot imagine, that the brave countries and gardens which fill the American hemisphere, were made for nothing but a place for dragons. . . . O New England, there is room to hope, that thou shalt belong to the City."

EDITOR'S NOTE

When the *Magnalia* was published, Cotton Mather was much pleased with the remark of an English reader that abridgment of the work was quite impossible: "No man that has relish for piety or variety can ever weary of reading it." This has by no means been the general verdict of later generations.

This book is an abridgment of the American edition published in 1852. Since that edition is in two volumes, each of which runs to over six hundred pages, the radical condensation of the present publication is apparent. Yet the structure of the original lends itself to selective excerpting and its style admits of judicious compression. The original ordering of the work into seven books has been preserved, but Mather's chapter divisions have generally been eliminated and new subheads have been introduced. The author's extensive capitalization and italicization have been largely omitted, but his orthography, word order, and phrasing have not been altered. The editor has in all cases attempted to convey a just impression of the organization and flavor of this American classic.

It is a pleasure to acknowledge the bibliographical assistance and editorial suggestions of my former students, Messrs. Thomas Barile, Francis Bremer, and Joseph McCormack.

See p 148 for the editor's Selected Bibliography.

CONTENTS

A GENERAL INTRODUCTION

I write the Wonders of the Christian Religion, flying from the depravations of Europe, to the American strand; and, assisted by the Holy Author of that Religion, I do with all conscience of truth, required therein by Him, who is the Truth itself, report the wonderful displays of His infinite power, wisdom, goodness, and faithfulness, wherewith His Divine Providence hath irradiated an Indian Wilderness.

I relate the considerable matters, that produced and attended the first settlement of colonies, which have been renowned for the degree of Reformation, professed and attained by evangelical churches, erected in those ends of the earth; and a field being thus prepared, I proceed unto a relation of the considerable matters which have been acted thereupon.

I first introduce the actors, that have in a more exemplary manner served those colonies; and give remarkable occurrences, in the exemplary lives of many magistrates, and of more ministers, who so lived as to leave unto posterity examples worthy of everlasting remembrance.

I add hereunto, the notables of the only Protestant university that ever shone in that hemisphere of the New World; with particular instances of Criolians,[1] in our biography, provoking the whole world with virtuous objects of emulation.

I introduce then, the actions of a more eminent importance, that have signalized those colonies: whether the establishments, directed by their synods; with a rich variety of synodical and ecclesiastical determinations; or, the disturbances, with which they have been from all sorts of temptations and enemies tempestuated; and the methods by which they have still weathered out each horrible tempest.

And into the midst of these actions, I interpose an entire book, wherein there is, with all possible veracity, a collection made of memorable occurrences, and amazing judgments and mercies befalling many particular persons among the people of New England.

Let my readers expect all that I have promised them, in this bill of fare; and it may be they will find themselves entertained with yet many other passages, above and beyond their expectation, deserving likewise a room in History: in all which, there will be nothing but the author's too mean way of preparing so great entertainments, to reproach the invitation.

The reader will doubtless desire to know, what it was that

> *tot Volvere casus*
> *Insignes Pictate Viros, tot adire Labores,*
> *Impulerit.*[2]

And our History shall, on many fit occasions which will be therein offered, endeavor, with all historical fidelity and simplicity, and with as little offence as may be, to satisfy him. The sum of the matter is, that from the very beginning of the Reformation in the English nation, there hath always been a generation of godly men, desirous to pursue the Reformation of religion, according to the Word of God, and the example of the best Reformed Churches; and answering the character of good men, given by Josephus, in his paraphrase on the words of Samuel to Saul, μηδεν ἀλλ'πξάχθῆσθαι καλῶσ ὑφ'ἑαυτῶν νομιζοντεσ, ἥ ὅ τι ἄν ποιήσωσι τοῦ Θεοῦ κεκελεύκοτοσ (They think they do nothing right in the service of God, but what they do ˙according to the command of God.) And there hath been another generation of men, who have still employed the power which they have generally still had in their hands, not only to stop the progress of the desired Reformation, but also, with innumerable vexations, to persecute those that most heartily wished well unto it. There were many of the Reformers, who joyned with the Reverend John Fox, in the complaints which he then entred in his Martyrology, about the "baits of Popery" yet left in the Church; and in his wishes, "God take them away, or ease us from them, for God knows they be the cause of much blindness and strife amongst men!" They zealously decreed the policy of complying always with the ignorance and vanity of the people; and cried out earnestly for purer administrations in the house of God, and more conformity to the law of Christ and primitive Christianity: while others would not hear of going any further than the first essay of Reformation. 'Tis very certain, that the first Reformers never intended that what they did should be the absolute boundary of Reformation, so that it should be a sin to proceed any further; as, by their own going beyond Wicklift, and changing and growing in their own models also, and the confessions of Cranmer, with the *Scripta Anglicana* of Bucer, and a thousand other things, was abundantly demonstrated. But after a fruitless expectation, wherein the truest friends of the Reformation long waited for to have that which Heylin himself owns to have been the design of the first Reformers, followed as it should have been, a party very unjustly arrogating to themselves the venerable name of the Church of England, by numberless oppressions, greviously smote those their fellow-servants. Then 'twas that, as our great Owen hath expressed it, "Multitudes of pious, peaceable Protestants, were driven, by their severities, to leave their native country, and seek a refuge for their lives and liberties, with freedom for the worship of God, in a wilderness in the ends of the earth."

It is the history of these Protestants that is here attempted: Protestants that highly honoured and affected the Church of England, and humbly petition to be a part of it: but by the mistake of a few powerful brethren, driven to seek a place for the exercise of the Protestant Religion, according to the light of their consciences, in the desarts of America. And in this attempt I have proposed, not only to preserve and secure the interest of religion in the churches of that little country New England, so far as the Lord Jesus Christ may please to bless it for that end, but also to offer unto the churches of the Reformation, abroad in the world, some small memorials, that may be serviceable unto the designs of reformation, whereto, I believe, they are quickly to be awakened. I am far from any such boast, concerning these churches, that they have need of nothing; I wish their works were more perfect before God. Nevertheless, I perswade myself, that so far as they have attained, they have given great examples of the methods and measures wherein an evangelical reformation is to be prosecuted, and of the qualifications requisite in the instruments that are to prosecute it, and of the difficulties which may be most likely to obstruct it, and the most likely directions and remedies for those obstructions. It may be, 'tis not possible for me to do a greater service unto the churches on the best island of the universe, than to give a distinct relation of those great examples which have been occurring among churches of exiles, that were driven out of that island, into an horrible wilderness, meerly for their being well-willers unto the Reformation. Thus, I do not say, that the churches of New England are the most regular that can be; yet I do say, and am sure, that they are very like unto those that were in the first ages of Christianity. And if I assert that, in the reformation of the Church, the state of it in those first Ages is to be not a little considered, the great Peter Ramus, among others, has emboldened me. For when the Cardinal of Lorrain, the Maecenas of that great man, was offended at him, for turning Protestant, he replied: *Inter Opes illas, quibus me ditasti, has etiam in oeternum recordabor, quod Beneficio Poessiaeac Responsionis tuae didici, de quindecim a Christo saeculis, primum vere esse aureum; Reliqua, quo longius abscederent, esse nequiora, atque deteriora: tum igitur cum fieret optio, Aureum saeculum delegi.*[3] In short, the first Age was the golden Age: to return unto that, will make a man a Protestant, and, I may add, a Puritan. 'Tis possible that our Lord Jesus Christ carried some thousands of reformers into the retirements of an American desart, on purpose that, with an opportunity granted unto many of his faithful servants, to enjoy the precious liberty of their ministry, though in the midst of many temptations all their days, He might there, to them first, and then by them, give a specimen of many good things, which He would have His churches elsewhere aspire and arise unto; and this being done, he knows not whether there be not all done, that New England was planted for; and whether the plantation may not, soon after this, come to nothing. Upon that expression in the sacred Scripture, "Cast the unprofitable servant into outer darkness," it hath been imagined by some, that the *Regiones exterae* of America, are the *Tenebrae exteriores,* which the unprofitable are there condemned unto. No doubt, the authors of those ecclesiastical impositions and severities, which drove the English Christians into the dark regions of America, esteemed those Christians to be a very unprofitable sort of creatures. But behold, ye European Churches, there are golden candlesticks (more than twice seven times seven!) in the midst of this "outer darkness:" unto the upright children of Abraham, here hath arisen light in darkness. And, let us humbly speak it, it shall be profitable for you to consider the light which, from the midst of this "outer darkness," is now to be darted over unto the other side of the Atlantick Ocean. But we must therewithal ask your prayers, that these "golden candlesticks" may not quickly be "removed out of their place!"

But whether New England may live any where else or no, it must live in our History! History, in general, hath had so many and mighty commendations from the pens of those numberless authors, who, from Herodotus to Howel, have been the professed writers of it, that a tenth part of them transcribed, would be a furniture for a *Polyanthea in folio.*[4] We, that have neither liberty, nor occasion, to quote these commendations of history, will content ourselves with the opinion of one who was not much of a professed historian, expressed in that passage, whereto all mankind subscribe, *Historia est Testis temporum, Nuntia vetustatis, Lux veritatis, vita memoriae, magistra vitae.*[5] But of all history it must be confessed, that the palm is to be given unto church history; wherein the dignity, the suavity, and the utility of the subject is transcendent. I observe, that for the description of the whole world in the Book of Genesis, that first-born of all historians, the great Moses, implies but one or two chapters, whereas he implies, it may be seven times as many chapters, in describing that one little pavil- lion, the Tabernacle. And when I am thinking what may be the reason of this difference, methinks it intimates unto us, that the Church wherein the service of God is performed, is much more precious than the world, which was indeed created for the sake and use of the Church. 'Tis very certain, that the greatest entertainments must needs occur in the history of the people whom the Son of God hath redeemed and purified unto himself, as a peculiar people, and whom the Spirit of God, by supernatural operations upon their minds, does cause to live like strangers in this world, conforming themselves unto the truths and rules of his Holy Word, in expectation of a Kingdom, whereto they shall be in another and a better World advanced. Let any person of good sense peruse the History of Herodotus, which, like a river taking rise where the sacred records of the Old Testament leave off, runs along smoothly and sweetly, with relations that sometimes perhaps want an apology, down until the Grecians drive the Persians before them. Let him then peruse Thucydides, who, from acting, betook himself to writing, and carries the ancient state of the Grecians down to the twenty-first year of the Pelopon- nesian wars, in a manner which Casaubon judges to be *Mirandum potius quam imitandum.*[6] Let him next revolve Xenophon, that "Bee of Athens," who continues a narra- tive of the Greek affairs from the Peloponnesian wars to the battle of Mantinea, and gives us a Cyrus into the bargain, at such a rate, that Lipsius reckons the character of a

Suavis, Fidus et Circumspectus Scriptor,[7] to belong unto him. Let him from hence proceed unto Diodorus Siculus, who, besides a rich treasure of Egyptian, Assyrian, Lybian and Grecian, and other antiquities, in a phrase which, according to Photius's judgment, is ἱστορια μαλιστα ὡρεῶκση (of all most becoming an historian), carries on the thread begun by his predecessors, until the end of the hundred and nineteenth Olympiad; and where he is defective, let it be supplied from Arrianus, from Justin, and from Curtius, who, in the relish of Colerus, is *Quovis melle dulcior.*[8] Let him hereupon, consult Polybius, and acquaint himself with the birth and growth of the Roman Empire, as far as 'tis described in five of the forty books composed by an author who, with a learned professor of history, is *Prudens Scriptor, si quis alius.*[9] Let him now run over the table of the Roman affairs, compendiously given by Lucius Florus, and then let him consider the transactions of above three hundred years reported by Dionysius Halicarnassaeus, who, if the censure of Bodin may be taken, *Graecos omnes et Latinos superasse videatur.*[10] Let him from hence pass to Livy, of whom the famous critick says, *Hoc solum ingenium (de Historicis Loquor) populus Romanus par Imperio suo habuit,*[11] and supply those of his *Decads* that are lost, from the best fragments of antiquity, in others (and especially Dion and Sallust) that lead us on still further in our way. Let him then proceed unto the writers of the Cesarean times, and first revolve Suetonius, then Tacitus, then Herodian, then a whole army more of historians which now crowd into our library; and unto all the rest, let him not fail of adding the incomparable Plutarch, whose books, they say, Theodore Gaza preferred before any in the world, next unto the inspired oracles of the Bible: but if the number be still too little to satisfie an historical appetite, let him add Polyhistor unto the number, and all the chronicles of the following ages. After all, he must sensibly acknowledge that the two short books of ecclesiastical history, written by the evangelist Luke, hath given us more

glorious entertainments than all these voluminous historians if they were put all together. The atchievements of
one Paul particularly, which that evangelist hath embla-
zoned, have more true glory in them, than all the acts of
those execrable plunderers and murderers, and irresistible
banditti of the world, which have been dignified by the
name of "conquerors." Tacitus counted *Ingentia bella,
expugnationes urbium, fusos captosque reges,*[12] the rages of
war, and the glorious violences, whereof great warriors make
a wretched ostentation, to be the noblest matter for an
historian. But there is a nobler, I humbly conceive, in the
planting and forming of evangelical churches, and the
temptations, the corruptions, the afflictions, which assault
them, and their salvations from those assaults, and the
exemplary lives of those that Heaven employs to be pat-
terns of holiness and usefulness upon earth: and unto such
it is, that I now invite my readers.

Reader! I have done the part of an impartial historian,
albeit not without all occasion perhaps, for the rule which
a worthy writer, in his *Historica,* gives to every reader,
*Historici legantur cum moderatione et venia, et cogitetur
fieri non posse ut in omnibus circumstantiis sint lyncei.*[13]
Polybius complains of those historians, who always made
either the Carthagenians brave, or the Romans base, or *e
contra,* in all their actions, as their affection for their own
party led them. I have endeavoured, with all good conscience, to decline this writing meerly for a party, or doing
like the dealer in history, whom Lucan derides, for always
calling the captain of his own party an Achilles, but of the
adverse party a Thersites: nor have I added unto the just
provocations for the complaint made by the Baron Mauri-
er, that the greatest part of histories are but so many
panegyricks composed by interested hands, which elevate
iniquity to the heavens, like Paterculus, and like Machiav-
el, who propose Tiberius Cesar, and Cesar Borgia, as examples fit for imitation, whereas true history would have
exhibited them as horrid monsters — as very devils. 'Tis

true, I am not of the opinion that one cannot merit the name of an impartial historian, except he write bare matters of fact without all reflection; for I can tell where to find this given as the definition of history, *Historia est rerum gestarum, cum laude aut vituperatione, narratio:*[14] and if I am not altogether a Tacitus, when vertues or vices occur to be matters of reflection, as well as of relation, I will, for my vindication, appeal to Tacitus himself, whom Lipsius calls one of the prudentest (though Tertullian, long before, counts him one of the lyingest) of them who have enriched the world with history: he says, *Praecipuum munus Annalium reor, ne virtutes sileantur, utque pravis Dictis, Factisque ex posteritate et Infamia metus sit.*[15] I have not commended any person, but when I have really judged, not only that he deserved it, but also that it would be a benefit unto posterity to know wherein he deserved it: and my judgment of desert, hath not been biassed by persons being of my own particular judgment, in matters of disputation, among the Churches of God. But whether I do myself commend, or whether I give my reader an opportunity to censure, I am careful above all things to do it with truth; and as I have considered the words of Plato, *Deum indigne et graviter ferre, cum quis ei similem, hoc est, virtute praestantem, vituperet, aut laudet contrarium:*[16] so I have had the Ninth Commandment of a greater law-giver than Plato, to preserve my care of truth from first to last. If any mistake have been any where committed, it will be found meerly circumstantial, and wholly involuntary. But although I thus challenge, as my due, the character of an impartial, I doubt I may not challenge that of an elegant historian. I cannot say whether the style wherein this Church-History is written, will please the modern criticks: but if I seem to have used αῶλκστατη συνταζει γραφησ,[17] a simple, submiss, humble style, 'tis the same that Eusebius affirms to have been used by Hegesippus, who, as far as we understand, was the first author (after Luke that ever composed an entire body of ecclesiastical history, which he divided into five books, and entituled, ὑπομνηματα των ἐκκληστικῶν πραξεων. 18 Whereas others, it may be, will reckon the style embellished with too much of ornament, by the multiplied references to other and former concerns, closely couched, for the observation of the attentive, in almost every paragraph; but I must confess, that I am of his mind who said, *Sicuti sal modice cibis aspersus Condit, et gratiam saporis addit, ita si paulum antiquitatis admiscueris, Oratio fit venustior.*19 And I have seldom seen that way of writing faulted, but by those who, for a certain odd reason, sometimes find fault that "the grapes are not ripe." These embellishments (of which yet I only — *Veniam pro laude peto*) 20 are not the puerile spoils of Polyanthea's; but I should have asserted them to be as choice flowers as most that occur in ancient or modern writings, almost unavoidably putting themselves into the author's hand, while about his work, if those words of Ambrose had not a little frighted me, as well as they did Baronius, *Unumquemque Fallunt sua scripta.*21 I observe that learned men have been so terrified by the reproaches of pedantry, which little smatterers at reading and learning have, for their quoting humours, brought upon themselves, that, for to avoid all approaches towards that which those feeble creatures have gone to imitate, the best way of writing has been most injuriously deserted. As for such unaccuracies as the critical may discover, *Opere in longo,*22 I appeal to the courteous for a favourable construction of them; and certainly they will be favourably judged of, when there is considered the variety of my other imployments; which have kept me in continual hurries, I had almost said like those of the ninth sphere, for the few months in which this work has been digesting.

Reader, I also expect nothing but scourges from that generation to whom the mass-book is dearer than the Bible: but I have now likewise confessed another expectation, that shall be my consolation under all. They tell us, that on the highest of the Capsian mountains, in Spain, there is a lake, whereinto if you throw a stone, there presently ascends a smoke which forms a dense cloud, from whence issues a tempest of rain, hail, and horrid thunderclaps for a good quarter of an hour. Our Church-History will be like a stone cast into that lake, for the furious tempest which it will raise among some, whose ecclesiastical dignities have set them as on the top of Spanish mountains. The catholick spirit of communion wherewith 'tis written, and the liberty which I have taken to tax the schismatical impositions and persecutions of a party who have always been as real enemies to the English nation as to the Christian and Protestant interest, will certainly bring upon the whole composure the quick censures of that party at the first cast of their look upon it.

But since an undertaking of this nature must thus encounter so much envy from those who are under the power of the spirit that works in the children of unperswadeableness, methinks I might perswade myself, that it will find another sort of entertainment from those good men who have a better spirit in them: for, as the Apostle James hath noted, "The spirit that is in us lusteth against envy;" and yet, even in us also, there will be the flesh, among whose works one is envy, which will be lusting against the spirit. All good men will not be satisfied with every thing that is here set before them. In my own country, besides a considerable number of loose and vain inhabitants risen up, to whom the Congregational church-discipline, which cannot live well where the power of godliness dyes, is become distasteful for the purity of it; there is also a number of eminently godly persons, who are for a larger way, and unto these my Church-History will give distaste, by the things which it may happen to utter in favour of that church-discipline on some few occasions; and the discoveries which I may happen to make of my apprehensions, that Scripture, and reason, and antiquity is for it; and that it is not far from a glorious resurrection. But that, as the famous Mr. Baxter, after thirty or forty years hard study, about the true instituted church-discipline, at last not only owned, but also invincibly proved, that it is the congregational; so, the further that the unprejudiced studies of learned men proceed in this matter, the more generally the Congregational church-discipline will be pronounced for. On the other side, there are some among us who very strictly profess the Congregational church-discipline, but at the same time they have an unhappy narrowness of soul, by which they confine their value and kindness too much unto their own party: and unto those my Church-History will be offensive, because my regard unto our own declared principles does not hinder me from giving the right hand of fellowship unto the valuable servants of the Lord Jesus Christ, who find not our church-discipline as yet agreeable unto their present understandings and illuminations. If it be thus in my own country, it cannot be otherwise in that whereto I send this account of my own. Briefly, as it hath been said, that if all Episcopal men were like Archbishop Usher, and all Presbyterians like Stephen Marshal, and all Independents like Jeremiah Burroughs, the wounds of the Church would soon be healed; my essay to carry that spirit through this whole Church-History, will bespeak wounds for it, from those that are of another spirit.

However, all these things, and an hundred more such things which I think of, are very small discouragements for such a service as I have here endeavoured. I foresee a recompence which will abundantly swallow up all discouragements! The recompence, whereof I do, with inexpressible joy, assure my self is this, that these my poor labours will certainly serve the Churches and interests of the Lord Jesus Christ. And I think I may say, that I ask to live no longer than I count a service unto the Lord Jesus Christ and his Churches, to be it self a glorious recompence for the doing of it.

Unto thee, therefore, O thou Son of God, and King of Heaven, and Lord of all things, whom all the glorious angels of light unspeakably love to glorifie; I humbly offer

up a poor History of Churches, which own thee alone for
their Head, and Prince, and Law-Giver; churches which
thou hast purchased with thy own blood, and with wonderful dispensations of thy Providence hitherto protected and
preserved; and of a people which thou didst form for thy
self; to shew forth thy praises. I bless thy great Name, for
thy inclining of me to, and carrying of me through, the
work of this History: I pray thee to sprinkle the book of
this History with thy blood, and make it acceptable and
profitable unto thy Churches, and serve thy truths and ways
among thy people, by that which thou hast here prepared;
for 'tis Thou that has prepared it for them. Amen.

Book I

ANTIQUITIES

Early discoveries in North America

It is the opinion of some, though 'tis but an opinion, and but of some learned men, that when the sacred oracles of Heaven assure us, the things under the earth are some of those, whose knees are to bow in the name of Jesus, by those things are meant the inhabitants of America, who are Antipodes to those of the other hemisphere. I would not quote any words of Lactantius, though there are some to countenance this interpretation, because of their being so ungeographical: nor would I go to strengthen the interpretation by reciting the words of the Indians to the first white invaders of their territories, we hear you are come from under the world to take our world from us. But granting the uncertainty of such an exposition, I shall yet give the Church of God a certain account of those things, which in America have been believing and adoring the glorious name of Jesus; and of that country in America, where those things have been attended with circumstances most remarkable. I can contentedly allow that America (which, as the learned Nicholas Fuller observes, might more justly be called Columbina) was altogether unknown to the penmen of the Holy Scriptures, and in the ages when the Scriptures were penned. I can allow, that those parts of the earth, which do not include America, are, in the inspired writings of Luke and of Paul, stiled all the world. I can allow, that the opinion of Torniellus and of Pagius, about the apostles preaching the gospel in America, has been sufficiently refuted by Basnagius. But I am out of the reach of Pope

Zachary's excommunication. I can assert the existence of the American Antipodes: and I can report unto the European churches great occurrences among these Americans. Yet I will report every one of them with such a Christian and exact veracity, that no man shall have cause to use about any one of them the words which the great Austin (as great as he was) used about the existence of Antipodes; it is a fable, and *nulla ratione credendum.*[23]

If the wicked one in whom the whole world lyeth, were he, who like a dragon, keeping a guard upon the spacious and mighty orchards of America, could have such a fascination upon the thoughts of mankind, that neither this balancing half of the globe should be considered in Europe, till a little more than two hundred years ago, nor the clue that might lead unto it, namely, the loadstone, should be known, till a Neapolitian stumbled upon it, about an hundred years before; yet the overruling providence of the great God is to be acknowledged, as well in the concealing of America for so long a time, as in the discovering of it, when the fulness of time was come for the discovery: for we may count America to have been concealed, while mankind in the other hemisphere had lost all acquaintance with it, if we may conclude it had any from the words of Diodorus Siculus, that Phoenecians were, by great storms, driven on the coast of Africa, far westward, ἐπι πολλασ ἡμεζασ, for many days together, and at last fell in with an island of prodigious magnitude; or from the words of Plato, that beyond the pillars of Hercules there was an island in the Atlantick Ocean, αμα λιβνησ και Ασιασ μειζων, larger than Africa and Asia put together: nor should it pass without remark, that three most memorable things, which have born a very great aspect upon humane affairs, did, near the same time, namely, at the conclusion of the fifteenth, and the beginning of the sixteenth century, arise unto the world: the first was the resurrection of literature; the second was the opening of America; the third was the Reformation of Religion. But, as probably, the devil seducing the first inhabitants of America into it, therein aimed at the having of them and their posterity out of the sound of the silver trumpets of the Gospel, then to be heard through the Roman Empire; if the devil had any expectation, that by the peopling of America, he should utterly deprive any Europeans of the two benefits, literature and religion, which dawned upon the miserable world, one just before, the other just after, the first famed navigation hither, 'tis to be hoped he will be disappointed of that expectation. The Church of God must no longer be wrapped up in Strabo's cloak; geography must now find work for a Christianography in regions far enough beyond the bounds wherein the Church of God had, through all former ages, been circumscribed. Renowned Churches of Christ must be gathered where the ancients once derided them that looked for any inhabitants.

Whatever truth may be in that assertion of one who writes: "If we may credit any records besides the Scriptures, I know it might be said and proved well, that this New World was known, and partly inhabited by Britains, or by Saxons from England, three or four hundred years before the Spaniards coming thither;" which assertion is demonstrated from the discourses between the Mexicans and the Spaniards at their first arrival; and the Popish reliques, as well as British terms and words, which the Spaniards then found among the Mexicans, as well as from undoubted passages, not only in other authors, but even in the British anals also: nevertheless, mankind generally agree to give unto Christopher Columbus, a Genoese, the honour of being the first European that opened a way into these parts of the world. It was in the year 1492, that this famous man, acted by a most vehement and wonderful impulse, was carried into the northern regions of this vast hemisphere, which might more justly therefore have received its name from him, than from Americus Vesputius, a Florentine, who, in the year 1497, made a further detection of the more southern regions in this continent. So a world is now found

out, and the affairs of the whole world have been affected
by the finding of it. So the Church of our Lord Jesus Christ,
well compared unto a ship, is now victoriously sailing
round the globe after Sir Francis Drake's renowned ship,
called, *The Victory,* which could boast,

Prima ego velivolis ambivi cursibus orbem.[24]

And yet the story about Columbus himself must be correct-
ed from the information of De la Vega, that "one Sanchez,
a native of Helva in Spain, did before him find out these
regions." He tells us that Sanchez using to trade in a small
vessel to the Canaries, was driven by a furious and tedious
tempest over unto these western countries; and at his return he gave to Colon, or Columbus, an account of what he
had seen, but soon after died of a disease he had got on his
dangerous voyage. However, I shall expect my 'reader, e'er
long, to grant, that some things done since by Almighty
God for the English in these regions, have exceeded all that
has been hitherto done for any other nation: If this New
World were not found out first by the English; yet in those
regards that are of all the greatest, it seems to be found out
more for them than any other.

But indeed the two Cabots, father and son, under the
commission of our King Henry VII, entering upon their
generous undertakings in the year 1497, made further discoveries of America, than either Columbus or Vesputius; in
regard of which notable enterprizes, the younger of them
had very great honours by the Crown put upon him, till at
length he died in a good old age, in which old age King
Edward VI had allowed him an honourable pension. Yea,
since the Cabots, employed by the King of England, made a
discovery of this continent in the year 1497, and it was the
year 1498 before Columbus discovered any part of the
continent; and Vesputius came a considerable time after
both of them; I know not why the Spaniard should go
unrivalled in the claim of this New World, which from the
first finding of it is pretended unto. These discoveries of the
Cabots were the foundation of all the adventures, with

which the English nation have since followed the sun, and
served themselves into an acquaintance on the hither side
of the Atlantick Ocean.

The learned Joseph Mede conjectures that the American
hemisphere will escape the conflagration of the earth,
which we expect at the descent of our Lord Jesus Christ
from Heaven: and that the people here will not have a
share in the blessedness which the renovated world shall
enjoy, during the thousand years of holy rest promised unto
the Church of God: and that the inhabitants of these
regions, who were originally Scytheans, and therein a notable fulfilment of the prophecy, about the enlargement of
Japhet, will be the Gog and Magog whom the devil will
seduce to invade the New-Jerusalem, with an envious hope
to gain the angelical circumstances of the people there. All
this is but conjecture. However, I am going to give unto the
Christian reader an history of some feeble attempts made in
the American hemisphere to anticipate the state of the
New-Jerusalem, as far as the unavoidable vanity of human
affairs and influence of Satan upon them would allow of it;
and of many worthy persons whose posterity, if they make a
squadron in the fleets of Gog and Magog, will be apostates
deserving a room, and a doom with the legions of the grand
apostate, that will deceive the nations to that mysterious
enterprize.

History of Plymouth

A number of devout and serious Christians in the English
nation, finding the Reformation of the Church in that
nation, according to the Word of God, and the design of
many among the first Reformers, to labour under a sort of
hopeless retardation; they did, Anno 1602, in the north of
England, enter into a covenant, wherein expressing themselves desirous, not only to attend the worship of our Lord
Jesus Christ, with a freedom from humane inventions and
additions, but also to enjoy all the evangelical institutions
of that worship, they did like those Macedonians, that are

therefore by the Apostle Paul commended, "give themselves up, first unto God, and then to one another." These pious people finding that their brethren and neighbours in the Church of England, as then established by law, took offence at these their endeavours after a scriptural reformation; and being loth to live in the continual vexations which they felt arising from their non-conformity to things which their consciences accounted superstitious and unwarrantable, they peaceably and willingly embraced a banishment into the Netherlands; where they settled at the city of Leyden, about seven or eight years after their first combination.

The English Church had not been very long at Leyden, before they found themselves encountred with many inconveniences. They felt that they were neither for health, nor purse, nor language well accommodated; but the concern which they most of all had, was for their posterity. They saw, that whatever banks the Dutch had against the inroads of the sea, they had not sufficient ones against a flood of manifold profaneness. They could not with ten years' endeavour bring their neighbours particularly to any suitable observation of the Lord's Day; without which they knew that all practical religion must wither miserably. They beheld some of their children, by the temptations of the place, were especially given in the licentious ways of many young people, drawn into dangerous extravagancies. Moreover, they were very loth to lose their interest in the English nation; but were desirous rather to enlarge their King's dominions. They found themselves also under a very strong disposition of zeal, to attempt the establishment of Congregational Churches in the remote parts of the world; where they hoped they should be reached by the royal influence of their prince, in whose allegiance they chose to live and die; at the same time likewise hoping that the ecclesiasticks, who had thus driven them out of the kingdom into a New World, for nothing in the world but their non-conformity to certain rites, by the imposers confessed indifferent, would be ashamed ever to persecute them with any further molestations, at the distance of a thousand leagues. These reasons were deeply considered by the church; and after many deliberations, accompanied with the most solemn humiliations and supplications before the God of Heaven, they took up a resolution, under the conduct of Heaven, to remove into America; the opened regions whereof had now filled all Europe with reports.

On August 5, 1620, they set sail from Southampton; but if it shall as I believe it will, afflict my reader to be told what heart-breaking disasters befell them, in the very beginning of their undertaking, let him glorifie God, who carried them so well through their greater affliction.

They were by bad weather twice beaten back, before they came to the Land's end. But it was judged, that the badness of the weather did not retard them so much as the deceit of a master, who, grown sick of the voyage, made such pretences about the leakiness of his vessel, that they were forced at last wholly to dismiss that lesser ship from the service. Being now all stowed into one ship, on the sixth of September they put to sea; but they met with such terrible storms, that the principal persons on board had serious deliberations upon returning home again; however, after long beating upon the Atlantick Ocean, they fell in with the land at Cape Cod, about the ninth of November following, where going on shore they fell upon their knees, with many and hearty praises unto God, who had been their assurance, when they were afar off upon the sea, and was to be further so, now that they were come to the ends of the earth.

But why at this Cape? Here was not the port which they intended: this was not the land for which they had provided. There was indeed a most wonderful providence of God, over a pious and a praying people, in this disappointment! The most crooked way that ever was gone, even that of Israel's peregrination through the wilderness, may be called a right way, such was the way of this little Israel, now going into a wilderness.

Their design was to have sat down some where about Hudson's River; but some of their neighbours in Holland having a mind themselves to settle a plantation there, secretly and sinfully contracted with the master of the ship, employed for the transportation of these our English exiles, by a more northerly course, to put a trick upon them. 'Twas in the pursuance of this plot that not only the goods, but also the lives of all on board were now hazarded, by the ships falling among the shoals of Cape-Cod; where they were so entangled among dangerous breakers, thus late in the year, that the company, got at last into the cape-harbour, broke off their intentions of going any further. And yet, behold the watchful providence of God over them that seek him! this false-dealing proved a safe-dealing for the good people against whom it was used. Had they been carried according to their desire unto Hudson's River, the Indians in those parts were at this time so many, and so mighty, and so sturdy, that in probability all this little feeble number of Christians had been massacred by these bloody savages, as not long after some others were: whereas the good hand of God now brought them to a country wonderfully prepared for their entertainment, by a sweeping mortality that had lately been among the natives.

Finding at their first arrival, that what other powers they had were made useless by the undesigned place of their arrival; they did, as the light of nature it self directed them, immediately in the harbour, sign an instrument, as a foundation of their future and needful government; wherein declaring themselves the loyal subjects of the Crown of England, they did combine into a body politick, and solemnly engage submission and obedience to the laws, ordinances, acts, constitutions and officers, that from time to time should be thought most convenient for the general good of the colony. This was done on Nov. 11th. 1620, and they chose one Mr. John Carver, a pious and prudent man, their governour.

The month of November being spent in many supplications to Almighty God, and consultations one with another, about the direction of their course; at last, on Dec. 6, 1620, they manned the shallop with about eighteen or twenty hands, and went out upon a third discovery. So bitterly cold was the season, that the spray of the sea lighting on their cloaths, glazed them with an immediate congelation; yet they kept cruising about the bay of Cape-Cod, and that night they got safe down the bottom of the bay. There they landed, and there they tarried that night; and unsuccessfully ranging about all the next day, at night they made a little *barricado* of boughs and logs, wherein the most weary slept. The next morning, after prayers, they suddenly were surrounded with a crue of Indians, who let fly a shower of arrows among them; whereat our distressed handful of English happily recovering their arms, which they had laid by from the moisture of the weather, they vigorously discharged their muskets upon the salvages, who astonished at the strange effects of such dead-doing things, as powder and shot, fled apace into the woods; but not one of ours was wounded by the Indian arrows that flew like hail about their ears, and pierced through sundry of their coats; for which they returned their solemn thanks unto God their Saviour; and they called the place by the name of, The First Encounter. From hence they coasted along, till an horrible storm arose, which tore their vessel at such a rate, and threw them into the midst of such dangerous breakers, it was reckoned little short of miracle that they escaped alive. In the end they got under the lee of a small island, where, going ashore, they kindled fires for their succour against the wet and cold; it was the morning before they found it was an island, whereupon they rendered their praises to Him that "hitherto had helped them;" and the day following, which was the Lord's day, the difficulties now upon them did not hinder them from spending it in the devout and pious exercises of a sacred rest. On the next day they sounded the harbour, and found it fit for shipping; they visited the main land also, and found it accommodated with pleasant fields and brooks; whereof they carried an encouraging report unto their friends on board. So they resolved that they would here pitch their tents; and sailing up to the town of Plymouth, (as with an hopeful *prolepsis,* my reader shall now call it; for otherwise, by the Indians 'twas called Patuxet;) on the twenty-fifth day of December they began to erect the first house that ever was in that memorable town.

If the reader would know, how these good people fared the rest of the melancholy winter, let him know, that besides the exercises of religion, with other work enough, there was the care of the sick to take up no little part of their time. 'Twas a most heavy trial of their patience, whereto they were called the first winter of this their pilgrimage, and enough to convince them and remind them that they were but Pilgrims. But what a wonder was it that all the bloody salvages far and near did not cut off this little remnant! If he that once muzzled the lions ready to devour the man of desires, had not admirably, I had almost said, miraculously restrained them, these had been all devoured! but this people of God were come into a wilderness to worship Him; and so He kept their enemies from such attempts, as would otherwise have soon annihilated this poor handful of men, thus far already diminished.

The doleful winter broke up sooner than was usual. But our crippled planters were not more comforted with the early advance of the spring, than they were surprized with the appearance of two Indians, who in broken English bade them, welcome Englishmen! It seems that one of these Indians had been in the eastern parts of New-England, acquainted with some of the English vessels that had been formerly fishing there; but the other of the Indians, and he from whom they had most of service, was a person provided by the very singular providence of God for that service. A most wicked ship-master being on this coast a few years before, had wickedly spirited away more than twenty Indians; whom having enticed them aboard, he presently stowed them under hatches, and carried them away to the Streights, where he sold as many of them as he could for slaves. The Indians would never forget or forgive this injury; but when the English afterwards came upon this coast, in their fishing-voyages, they were still assaulted in an hostile manner, to the killing and wounding of many poor men by the angry natives, in revenge of the wrong that had been done them; and some intended plantations here were hereby utterly nipt in the bud. But our good God so ordered it, that one of the stolen Indians, called Squanto, had escaped out of Spain into England; where he lived with one Mr. Slany, from whom he had found a way to return into his own country, being brought back by one Mr. Dermer, about half a year before our honest Plymotheans were cast upon this continent. This Indian (with the other) having received much kindness from the English, who he saw generally condemned the man that first betrayed him, now made unto the English a return of that kindness: and being by his acquaintance with the English language, fitted for a conversation with them, he very kindly informed them what was the present condition of the Indians; instructed them in the way of ordering their corn; and acquainted them with many other things, which it was necessary for them to understand. But Squanto did for them a yet greater benefit than all this: for he brought Massasoit, the chief Sachim or Prince of the Indians within many miles, with some scores of his attenders, to make our people a kind visit; the issue of which visit was, that Massasoit not only entred into a firm agreement of peace with the English, but also they declared and submitted themselves to be subjects of the King of England; into which peace and subjection many other sachims quickly after came, in the most voluntary manner that could be expressed.

Setting aside the just and great grief of our new planters for the immature death of their excellent governour, succeeded by the worthy Mr. Bradford, early in the spring after their first arrival, they spent their summer somewhat comfortably, trading with the Indians to the northward of their plantation; in which trade they were not a little assisted by Squanto, who within a year or two dyed among the English; but before his death, desired them to pray for him, that he might go to the Englishman's God in Heaven. And besides the assistance of Squanto, they had also the help of another Indian, called Hobbamok, who continued faithful unto the English interests as long as he lived; though he sometimes went in danger of his life among his countrymen for that fidelity. So they jogged on till the day twelvemonth after their first arrival; when there now arrived unto them a good number more of their old friends from Holland, for the strengthening of their new plantation; but inasmuch as they brought not a sufficient stock of provisions with them, they rather weakened it, than strengthened it.

In one of the first summers after their sitting down at Plymouth, a terrible drought threatened the ruin of all their summer's husbandry. From about the middle of May to the middle of July, an extream hot sun beat upon their fields, without any rain, so that all their corn began to wither and languish, and some of it was irrecoverably parched up. In this distress they set apart a day for fasting and prayer, to deprecate the calamity that might bring them to fasting through famine; in the morning of which day there was no sign of any rain; but before the evening the sky was overcast with clouds, which went not away without such easie, gentle, and yet plentiful showers, as revived a great part of their decayed corn, for a comfortable harvest. The Indians themselves took notice of this answer given from heaven to the supplications of this devout people; and one of them said, "Now I see that the Englishman's God is a good God; for he hath heard you, and sent you rain, and that without such tempest and thunder as we use to have with our rain; which after our Powawing for it, breaks down the corn; whereas your corn stands whole and good still; surely, your God is a good God." The harvest which God thus gave to this pious people, caused them to set apart another day for solemn Thanksgiving to the glorious Hearer of Prayers!

After these many difficulties were thus a little surmounted, the inhabitants of this colony prosecuted their affairs at so vigorous and successful a rate, that they not only fell into a comfortable way, both of planting and of trading; but also in a few years there was a notable number of towns to be seen settled among them, and very considerable churches, walking, so far as they had attained, in the faith and order of the Gospel. Their churches flourished so considerably, that in the year 1642, there were above a dozen ministers, and some of those ministers were stars of the first magnitude, shining in their several orbs among them. And as they proceeded in the evangelical service and worship of our Lord Jesus Christ, so they prospered in their secular concernments. When they first began to divide their lands, they wisely contrived the division so, that they might keep close together for their mutual defence; and then their condition was very like that of the Romans in the time of Romulus, when every man contented himself with two acres of land; and, as Pliny tells us, "It was thought a great reward for one to receive a pint of corn from the people of Rome, which corn they also pounded in mortars." But since then their condition is marvellously altered and amended; great farms are now seen among the effects of this good people's planting; and in their fishing, from the catching of cod, and other fish of less dimentions, they are since passed on to the catching of whales, whose oil is become a staple-cômmodity of the country.

Some little controversies have now and then arisen among them in the administration of their discipline; but synods then regularly called, have usually and presently put into joint all that was apprehended out. Their chief hazard and symptom of degeneracy, is in the verification of that old observation, *Religio perperit Divitias, et filia devoravit matrem:* "Religion brought forth prosperity, and the daughter destroyed the mother." The one would expect, that as they grew in their estates, they would grow in the payment of their quit-rents unto the God who gives them power to get wealth, by more liberally supporting his ministers and ordinances among them; the most likely way to save them from the most miserable apostacy; the neglect whereof in some former years, began for a while to be punished with a sore famine of the Word; nevertheless, there is danger lest the enchantments of this world make them to forget their errand into the wilderness: and some woeful villages in the skirts of the colony, beginning to live without the means of grace among them, are still more ominous intimations of the danger. May the God of New-England preserve them from so great a death!

History of Massachusetts Bay

There were more than a few attempts of the English to people and improve the parts of New-England which were to the northward of New-Plymouth; but the designs of those attempts being aimed no higher than the advancement of some worldly interests, a constant series of disasters has confounded them, until there was a plantation erected upon the nobler designs of Christianity; and that plantation, though it has had more adversaries than perhaps any one upon earth; yet, "having obtained help from God, it continues to this day." There have been very fine settlements in the north-east regions; but what is become of them? I have heard that one of our ministers once preaching to a congregation there, urged them to approve themselves a religious people from this consideration, "that otherwise they would contradict the main end of planting this wilderness;" whereupon a well-known person, then in the assembly, cryed out, "Sir, you are mistaken: you think you are preaching to the people at the Bay; our main end was to catch fish." Truly, 'twere to have been wished, that something more excellent had been the main end of the settlements in that brave country, which we have, even long since the arrival of that more pious colony at the Bay, now seen dreadfully unsettled, no less than twice at least, by the sword of the heathen, after they had been replenished with many hundreds of people, who had thriven to many thousands of pounds; and had all the force of the Bay, too, to assist them in the maintaining of their settlements. But the same or the like inauspicious things attended many other endeavours to make plantations upon such a main end in several other parts of our country, before the arrival of those by whom the Massachuset colony was at last formed upon more glorious aims; all proving, like the habitations of the foolish, "cursed before they had taken root."

Several persons in the west of England, having by fishing-voyages to Cape Ann, the northern promontory of the Massachuset-Bay, obtained some acquaintance with those parts; the news of the good progress made in the new plantation of Plymouth, inspired the renowned Mr. White, minister of Dorchester, to prosecute the settlement of such another plantation here for the propagation of religion. This good man engaged several gentlemen about the year 1624, in this noble design; and they employed a most religious, prudent, worthy gentleman, one Mr. Roger Conant, in the government of the place, and of their affairs upon the place, but through many discouragements, the design for a while almost fell unto the ground. That great man, greatly grieved hereat, wrote over to this Mr. Roger Conant, that if he and three honest men more would yet stay upon the spot, he would procure a patent for them, and send them over friends, goods, provisions, and what was necessary to assist their undertakings. Mr. Conant, then looking out a scituation more commodious for a town, gave his three disheartened companions to understand, that he did believe God would make this land a receptacle for his people; and that if they should leave him, yet he would not stir; for he was confident he should not long want company; which confidence of his caused them to abandon the thoughts of leaving him.

Well, it was not long before the Council of Plymouth in England had, by a deed bearing date March 19, 1627, sold unto some knights and gentlemen about Dorchester, viz: Sir Henry Rowsel, Sir John Young, Thomas Southcott, John Humphrey, John Endicott, and Simon Whetcomb, and their heirs and assigns, and their associates for ever, that part of New-England which lyes between a great river called Merrimack, and a certain other river there called Charles' River, in the bottom of the Massachuset-Bay. But shortly after this, Mr. White brought the aforesaid honourable persons into an acquaintance with several other persons of quality about London; as, namely, Sir Richard Saltonstall, Isaac Johnson, Samuel Adderly, John Ven, Matthew Cradock, George Harwood, Increase Nowel, Richard Perry, Richard Bellingham, Nathaniel Wright, Samuel Vassal, Theophilus Eaton, Thomas Goff, Thomas Admas, John Brown, Samuel Brown, Thomas Hutchings, William Vassal, William Pinchon, and George Foxcraft. These persons being associated unto the former, and having bought of them all their interest in New-England aforesaid, now consulted about settling a plantation in that country, whither such as were then called Non-conformists might, with the grace and leave of the King, make a peaceable secession, and enjoy the liberty and the exercise of their own perswasions about the worship of the Lord Jesus Christ. Whereupon petitioning the King to confirm what they had thus purchased with a new patent, he granted them one, bearing date from the year 1628, which gave them a right unto the soil, holding their titles of lands, as of the mannor of East Greenwich in Kent, and in common soccage.

By this charter they were empowered yearly to elect their own governour, deputy-governour and magistrates; as also to make such laws as they should think suitable for the plantation: but as an acknowledgment of their dependance upon England, they might not make any laws repugnant unto those of the kingdom; and the fifth part of all the oar of gold or silver found in the territory, belonged unto the crown. So, soon after Mr. Cradock being by the company chosen governour, they sent over Mr. Endicott in the year 1628, to carry on the plantation, which the Dorchester-agents had lookt out for them, which was at a place called Nahumkeick. Of which place I have somewhere met with an odd observation, that the name of it was rather Hebrew than Indian; for נחום, *Nahum*, signifies comfort, and חוק, *Keik*, signifies an haven; and our English not only found it an haven of comfort, but happened also to put an Hebrew name upon it; for they called it Salem, for the peace which they had and hoped in it; and so it is called unto this day.

The report of the charter granted unto the governour and company of the Massachuset-Bay, and the entertainment and encouragement which planters began to find in that Bay, came with a — *Patrias age, desere Sedes*,[25] and caused many very deserving persons to transplant themselves and their families into New-England. Gentlemen of ancient and worshipful families, and ministers of the gospel, then of great fame at home, and merchants, husbandmen, artificers, to the number of some thousands, did for twelve years together carry on this transplantation. It was indeed a banishment rather than a removal, which was undergone by this glorious generation, and you may be sure sufficiently afflictive to men of estate, breeding and conversation. As the hazard which they ran in this undertaking was of such extraordinariness, that nothing less than a strange and strong impression from Heaven could have thereunto moved the hearts of such as were in it: so the expense with which they carried on the undertaking was truly extraordinary. About an hundred and ninety-eight ships were employed in passing the perils of the seas, in the accomplishment of this renowned settlement; whereof, by the way, but one miscarried in those perils.

Mr. Higginson, and Mr. Skelton, and other good people that arrived at Salem, in the year 1629, resolved, like their father Abraham, to begin their plantation with "calling on

the name of the Lord." The great Mr. Hildersham had
advised our first planters to agree fully upon their form of
church government, before their coming into New-
England; but they had indeed agreed little further than in
this general principle, "that the reformation of the church
was to be endeavoured according to the written word of
God." Accordingly ours, now arrived at Salem, consulted
with their brethren at Plymouth, what steps to take for the
more exact acquainting of themselves with, and conforming
themselves to, that written word; and the Plymotheans, to
their great satisfaction, laid before them what warrant, they
judged, that they had in the laws of our Lord Jesus Christ,
for every particular in their church-order.

Whereupon having the concurrence and countenance of
their deputy-governour, the worshipful John Endicott,
Esq., and the approving presence of the messengers from
the church of Plymouth, they set apart the sixth day of
August, after their arrival, for fasting and prayer, for the
settling of a church state among them, and for their making
a confession of their faith, and entering into an holy
covenant, whereby that church state was formed.

Mr. Higginson then became the teacher, and Mr. Skelton
the pastor, of the church thus constituted at Salem; and
they lived very peaceably in Salem together, till the death
of Mr. Higginson, which was about a twelve-month after,
and then of Mr. Skelton, who did not long survive him.

As for the circumstances of admission into this Church,
they left it very much unto the discretion and faithfulness
of their elders, together with the condition of the persons to
be admitted. Some were admitted by expressing their consent unto their confession and covenant; some were admitted after their first answering to questions about religion, propounded unto them; some were admitted, when
they had presented in writing such things as might give
satisfaction unto the people of God concerning them; and
some that were admitted, orally addressed the people of
God in such terms, as they thought proper to ask their

communion with; which diversity was perhaps more beautiful than would have been a more punctilious uniformity;
but none were admitted without regard unto a blameless
and holy conversation. They did all agree with their brethren of Plymouth in this point, "That the children of the
faithful were church-members, with their parents; and that
their baptism was a seal of their being so;" only before their
admission to fellowship in a particular church, it was
judged necessary that, being free from scandal, they should
be examined by the elders of the church, upon those
approbation of their fitness, they should publickly and
personally own the covenant; so they were to be received
unto the table of the Lord.

The Governour and Company of the Massachuset-Bay,
then in London, did in the year 1629, after exact and
mature debates, conclude, that it was most convenient for
the government, with the charter of the plantation, to be
transferred into the plantation it self; and an order of court
being drawn up for that end, there was then chosen a new
governour, and a new deputy-governour, that were willing
to remove themselves with their families thither on the first
occasion. The governour was John Winthrop, Esq., a
gentleman of that wisdom and virtue, and those manifold
accomplishments, that after-generations must reckon him
no less a glory, than he was a patriot of the country. The
deputy-governour was Thomas Dudley, Esq., a gentleman,
whose natural and acquired abilities, joined with his excellent moral qualities, entitled him to all the great respects
with which his country on all opportunities treated him.
Several most worthy assistants were at the same time chosen
to be in this transportation; moreover, several other gentlemen of prime note, and several famous ministers of the
gospel, now likewise embarked themselves with these
honourable adventurers; who equipped a fleet consisting of
ten or eleven ships, whereof the admiral was, The Arabella
(so called in honour of the right honourable the Lady
Arabella Johnson, at this time on board), a ship of three

hundred and fifty tuns; and in some of the said ships there were two hundred passengers; all of which arrived before the middle of July, in the year 1630, safe in the harbours of New-England.

But the most notable circumstance in their farewel, was their composing and publishing of what they called, "The humble request of his Majesties loyal subjects, the Governour and Company lately gone for New-England, to the rest of their brethren in and of the Church of England; for the obtaining of their prayers, and the removal of suspicions and misconstructions of their intentions." In this address of theirs, notwithstanding the trouble they had undergone for desiring to see the Church of England reformed of several things, which they thought its deformities, yet they now called the Church of England their dear mother; acknowledging that such hope and part as they had obtained in the common salvation they had sucked from her breasts; therewithal entreating their many reverend fathers and brethren to recommend them unto the mercies of God, in their constant prayers, as a church now springing out of their own bowels.

Being happily arrived at New-England, our new planters found the difficulties of a rough and hard wilderness presently assaulting them: of which the worst was the sickliness which many of them had contracted by their other difficulties. The mortality thus threatning of this new plantation so enlivened the devotions of this good people, that they set themselves by fasting and prayer to obtain from God the removal of it; and their brethren at Plymouth also attended the like duties on their behalf: the issue whereof was, that in a little time they not only had health restored, but they likewise enjoyed the special directions and assistance of God in the further prosecution of their undertakings.

But there were two terrible distresses more, besides that of sickness, whereto this people were exposed in the beginning of their settlement: though a most seasonable and almost unexpected mercy from Heaven still rescued them out of those distresses. One thing that sometimes extreamly exercised them, was a scarcity of provisions; in which 'twas wonderful to see their dependance upon God, and God's mindfulness of them. When the parching droughts of the summer divers times threatened them with an utter and a total consumption to the fruits of the earth, it was their manner, with heart-melting, and I may say, Heaven-melting devotions to fast and pray before God; and on the very days when they poured out the water of their tears before him, he would shower down the water of his rain upon their fields; while they were yet speaking, he would hear them; insomuch that the salvages themselves would on that occasion admire the Englishman's God!

Another thing that gave them no little exercise, was the fear of the Indians, by whom they were sometimes alarmed. But this fear was wonderfully prevented, not only by intestine wars happening then to fall out among those barbarians, but chiefly by the small-pox, which proved a great plague unto them, and particularly to one of the princes of the Massachuset-bay, who yet seemed hopefully to be christianized before he dyed. This distemper getting in, I know not how, among them, swept them away with a most prodigious desolation, insomuch that although the English gave them all the assistances of humanity in their calamities, yet there was, it may be, not one in ten among them left alive; of those few that lived, many also fled from the infection, leaving the country a meer Golgotha of unburied carcases; and as for the rest, the English treated them with all the civility imaginable; among the instances of which civility, let this be reckoned for one, that notwithstanding the patent which they had for the country, they fairly purchased of the natives the several tracts of land which they afterwards possessed.

The people in the fleet that arrived at New-England, in the year 1630, left the fleet almost, as the family of Noah did the ark, having a whole world before them to be peopled. Salem was already supplied with a competent number of inhabitants; and therefore the governour, with most of the gentlemen that accompanied him in his voyage, took their first opportunity to prosecute further settlements about the bottom of the Massachuset-Bay; but where-ever they sat down, they were so mindful of their errand into the wilderness, that still one of their first works was to gather a church into the covenant and order of the gospel. First, there was a church thus gathered at Charles-town, on the north side of Charles's River; where, keeping a solemn fast on August 27, 1630, to implore the conduct and blessing of Heaven on their ecclesiastical proceedings, they chose Mr. Wilson, a most holy and zealous man, formerly a minister of Sudbury, in the county of Suffolk, to be their teacher; and although he now submitted unto an ordination, with an imposition of such hands as were by the church invited so to pronounce the benediction of Heaven upon him; yet it was done with a protestation by all, that it should be only as a sign of his election to the charge of his new flock, without any intention that he should thereby renounce the ministry he had received in England. After the gathering of the church at Charles-town, there quickly followed another at the town of Dorchester.

And after Dorchester there followed another at the town of Boston, which issued out of Charles-town; one Mr. James took the care of the church at Charles-town, and Mr. Wilson went over to Boston, where they that formerly belonged unto Charles-town, with universal approbation became a distinct church of themselves. To Boston soon succeeded a church at Roxbury; to Roxbury, one at Lyn; to Lyn, one at Watertown; so that in one or two years' time there were to be seen seven churches in this neighborhood, all of them attending to what the spirit if the Scripture said unto them; all of them golden candlesticks, illustrated with a very sensible presence of our Lord Jesus Christ among them.

It was for a matter of twelve years together, that persons of all ranks, well affected unto church-reformation, kept sometimes dropping, and sometimes flocking into New-

England, though some that were coming into New-England were not suffered so to do. However, the number of those who did actually arrive at New-England before the year 1640, have been computed about four thousand; since which time far more have gone out of the country than have come to it; and yet the God of Heaven so smiled upon the plantation, while under an easie and equal government, the designs of Christianity in well-formed churches have been carried on, that no history can parallel it.

Never was any plantation brought unto such a considerableness, in a space of time so inconsiderable! an howling wilderness in a few years became a pleasant land, accommodated with the necessaries — yea, and the conveniences of humane life; the gospel has carried with it a fulness of all other blessings; and (albeit, that mankind generally, as far as we have any means of enquiry, have increased in one and the same given proportion, and so no more than doubled themselves in about three hundred and sixty years, in all the past ages of the world, since the fixing of the present period of humane life) the four thousand first planters, in less than fifty years, notwithstanding all transportations and mortalities, increased into, they say, more than an hundred thousand.

History of the Later New England Colonies

It was not long before the Massachuset Colony was become like an hive overstocked with bees; and many of the new inhabitants entertained thoughts of swarming into plantations extended further into the country. The fame of Connecticut river, a long, fresh, rich river, (as indeed the name Connecticut is Indian for a long river,) had made a little *Nilus*,[26] of it in the expectations of the good people about the Massachuset-bay: whereupon many of the planters belonging especially to the towns of Cambridge, Dorchester, Watertown and Roxbury, took up resolutions to travel an hundred miles westward from those towns, for a further settlement upon this famous river.

It was in the year 1635, that this design was first formed;

and the disposition of the celebrated Mr. Thomas Hooker, with his people now in Cambridge, to engage in the design, was that which gave most life unto it. They then sent their agents to view the country, who returned with so advantageous a report, that the next year there was a great remove of good people thither: on this remove, they that went from Cambridge became a church upon a spot of ground now called Hartford; they that went from Dorchester, became a church at Windsor; they that went from Watertown, sat down at Wethersfield; and they that left Roxbury were inchurched higher up the river at Springfield, a place which was afterwards found within the line of the Massachuset-charter. Indeed, the first winter after their going thither, proved an hard one; and the grievous disappointments which befel them, through the unseasonable freezing of the river, whereby their vessel of provisions was detained at the mouth of the river, three-score miles below them, caused them to encounter with very disastrous difficulties. Divers of them were hereby obliged in the depth of winter to travel back into the Bay; and some of them were frozen to death in the journey.

However, such was their courage, that they prosecuted their plantation-work with speedy and blessed successes; and when bloddy salvages in their neighbourhood, known by the name of Pequots, had like to have nipt the plantation in the bud, by a cruel war, within a year or two after their settlement, the marvellous providence of God immediately extinguished that war, by prospering the New-English arms, unto the utter subduing of the quarrelsome nation, and affrightning of all the other natives.

It was with the countenance and assistance of their brethren in the Massachuset-bay, that the first planters of Connecticut made their essays thus to discover and cultivate the remoter parts of this mighty wilderness; and accordingly several gentlemen went furnished with some kind of commission from the government of the Massachuset-bay, for to maintain some kind of government among the inhabitants, till there could be a more orderly settlement. But the inhabitants quickly perceiving themselves to be without the line of the Massachuset-charter, entered into a combination among themselves, whereby with mutual consent they became a body-politick, and framed a body of necessary laws and orders, to the execution whereof they chose all necessary officers, very much, though not altogether, after the form of the colony from whence they issued.

The church-order observed in the churches of Connecticut, has been the same that is observed by their sisters in the Massachuset-bay; and in this order they lived exceeding peaceably all the eleven years that Mr. Hooker lived among them. Nevertheless there arose at length some unhappy contests in one town of the colony, which grew into an alienation that could not be cured without such a parting, and yet, indeed, hardly so kind a parting, as that whereto once Abraham and Lot were driven. However, these little, idle, angry controversies, proved occasions of enlargements to the church of God; for such of the inhabitants as chose a cottage in a wilderness, before the most beautiful and furnished edifice, overheated with the fire of contention, removed peaceably higher up the river, where a whole county of holy churches has been added unto the number of our congregations.

But there was one thing that made this colony to become very considerable; which thing remains now to be considered. The well-known Mr. Davenport, and Mr. Eaton, and several eminent persons that came over to the Massachuset-bay among some of the first planters, were strongly urged, that they would have settled in this Bay; but hearing of another Bay to the south-west of Connecticut, which might be more capable to entertain those that were to follow them, they desired that their friends at Connecticut would purchase of the native proprietors for them, all the land that lay between themselves and Hudson's River, which was in part effected. Accordingly removing thither in the year 1637, they seated themselves in a pleasant bay, where they spread themselves along the seacoast, and one might have been suddenly as it were surprized with the sight of such notable towns, as first New-Haven; then Guilford; then Milford; then Stamford; and then Brainford, where our Lord Jesus Christ is worshipped in churches of an evangelical constitution; and from thence, if the enquirer make a salley over to Long-Island, he might there also have seen the churches of our Lord beginning to take root in the eastern parts of that island. All this while this fourth colony wanted the legal basis of a charter to build upon; but they did by mutual agreement form themselves, into a body-politick as like as they judged fit unto the other colonies in their neighbourhood; and as for there church-order, it was generally *secundum usum Massachusettensem*.[27]

But what is now become of New-Haven colony? I must answer, It is not: and yet it has been growing ever since it first was. But when Connecticut-colony petitioned the restored King for a charter, they procured New-Haven colony to be annexed unto them in the same charter; and this, not without having first the private concurrence of some leading men in the colony; though the minds of others were so uneasie about the coalition, that it cost some time after the arrival of the charter for the colony, like Jephtha's daughter to bewail her condition, before it could be quietly complied withal. Nevertheless they have lived ever since, one colony, very happily together, and the God of love and peace has remarkably dwelt among them: however, these children of God have not been without their chastisements, especially in the malignant fevers and agues, which have often proved very mortal in most or all of their plantations.

But thus was the settlement of New-England brought about; these were the beginnings, these the foundations of those colonies, which have not only enlarged the English empire in some regards more than any other outgoings of our nation, but also afforded a singular prospect of churches erected in an American corner of the world, on purpose to express and pursue the Protestant Reformation.

Book II

THE SHIELDS OF THE CHURCHES:
NEW ENGLAND'S GOVERNORS

Life of William Bradford

It has been a matter of some observation, that although Yorkshire be one of the largest shires in England; yet, for all the fires of martyrdom which were kindled in the days of Queen Mary, it afforded no more fuel than one poor Leaf; namely, John Leaf, an apprentice, who suffered for the doctrine of the Reformation at the same time and stake with the famous John Bradford. But when the reign of Queen Elizabeth would not admit the Reformation of worship to proceed unto those degrees, which were proposed and pursued by no small number of the faithful in those days, Yorkshire was not the least of the shires in England that afforded suffering witnesses thereunto. The churches there gathered were quickly molested with such a raging persecution, that if the spirit of separation in them did carry them unto a further extream than it should have done, one blameable cause thereof will be found in the extremity of that persecution. Their troubles made that cold country too hot for them, so that they were under a necessity to seek a retreat in the Low Countries; and yet the watchful malice and fury of their adversaries rendred it almost impossible for them to find what they sought. For them to leave their native soil, their lands and their friends, and go into a strange place, where they must hear foreign language, and live meanly and hardly, and in other imployments than that of husbandry, wherein they had been educated, these must needs have been such discouragements as could have been conquered by none, save those who "sought first the kingdom of God, and the righteousness thereof." But that which would have made these discouragements the more unconquerable unto an ordinary faith, was the terrible zeal of their enemies to guard all ports, and search all ships, that none of them should be carried off.

I will not relate the sad things of this kind then seen and felt by this people of God; but only exemplifie those trials with one short story. Divers of this people having hired a Dutchman, then lying at Hull, to carry them over to Holland, he promised faithfully to take them in between Grimsly and Hull; but they coming to the place a day or two too soon, the appearance of such a multitude alarmed the officers of the town adjoining, who came with a great body of soldiers to seize upon them. Now it happened that one boat full of men had been carried aboard, while the women were yet in a bark that lay aground in a creek at low water. The Dutchman perceiving the storm that was thus beginning ashore, swore by the sacrament that he would stay no longer for any of them; and so taking the advantage of a fair wind then blowing, he put out to sea for Zealand. The women thus left near Grimsly-common, bereaved of their husbands, who had been hurried from them, and forsaken of their neighbours, of whom none durst in this fright stay with them, were a very rueful spectacle; some crying for fear, some shaking for cold, all dragged by troops of armed and angry men from one justice to another, till not knowing what to do with them, they even dismissed them to shift as well as they could for themselves. But by their singular afflictions, and by their Christian behaviours, the cause for which they exposed themselves did gain considerably.

In the mean time, the men at sea found reason to be glad that their families were not with them, for they were surprized with an horrible tempest, which held them for fourteen days together, in seven whereof they saw not sun, moon or star, but were driven upon the coast of Norway. The mariners often despaired of life, and once with doleful shrieks gave over all, as thinking the vessel was foundred: but the vessel rose again, and when the mariners with sunk hearts often cried out, "We sink! We sink!" the passengers, without such distraction of mind, even while the water was running into their mouths and ears, would chearfully shout, "Yet, Lord, thou canst save! Yet, Lord, thou canst save!" And the Lord accordingly brought them at last safe unto their desired haven: and not long after helped their distressed relations thither after them, where indeed they found upon almost all accounts a new world, but a world in which they found that they must live like strangers and pilgrims.

Among those devout people was our William Bradford, who was born *Anno* 1588, in an obscure village called Ansterfield, where the people were as unacquainted with the Bible, as the Jews do seem to have been with part of it in the days of Josiah; a most ignorant and licentious people, and like unto their priest. Here, and in some other places, he had a comfortable inheritance left him of his honest parents, who died while he was yet a child, and cast him on the education, first of his grand parents, and then of his uncles, who devoted him, like his ancestors, unto the affairs of husbandry. Soon a long sickness kept him, as he would afterwards thankfully say, from the vanities of youth, and made him the fitter for what he was afterwards to undergo. When he was about a dozen years old, the reading of the Scriptures began to cause great impressions upon him; and those impressions were much assisted and improved, when he came to enjoy Mr. Richard Clifton's illuminating ministry, not far from his abode; he was then also further befriended, by being brought into the company and fellowship of such as were then called professors; though the young man that brought him into it did after become a prophane and wicked apostate. Nor could the wrath of his uncles, nor the scoff of his neighbours, now turned upon him, as one of the Puritans, divert him from his pious inclinations.

Some lamented him, some derided him, all disswaded him: nevertheless, the more they did it, the more fixed he was in his purpose to seek the ordinances of the gospel, where they should be dispensed with most of the commanded purity; and the sudden deaths of the chief relations which thus lay at him, quickly after convinced him what a folly it had been to have quitted his profession, in expectation of any satisfaction from them. So to Holland he attempted a removal.

Having with a great company of Christians hired a ship to transport them for Holland, the master perfidiously betrayed them into the hands of those persecutors, who rifled and ransacked their goods, and clapped their persons into prison at Boston, where they lay for a month together. But Mr. Bradford being a young man of about eighteen, was dismissed sooner than the rest, so that within a while he had opportunity with some others to get over to Zealand, through perils, both by land and sea not inconsiderable.

When the magistrates understood the true cause of his coming thither, they were well satisfied with him; and so he repaired joyfully unto his brethren at Amsterdam, where the difficulties to which he afterwards stooped in learning and serving of a Frenchman at the working of silks, were abundantly compensated by the delight wherewith he sat under the shadow of our Lord, in his purely dispensed ordinances. At the end of two years, he did, being of age to do it, convert his estate in England into money; but setting up for himself, he found some of his designs by the providence of God frowned upon, which he judged a correction bestowed by God upon him for certain decays of internal piety, whereinto he had fallen; the consumption of his estate he thought came to prevent a comsumption in his virtue. But after he had resided in Holland about half a score years, he was one of those who bore a part in that hazardous and generous enterprise of removing into New-

England, with part of the English church at Leyden, where, at their first landing, his dearest consort accidentally falling overboard, was drowned in the harbour; and the rest of his days were spent in the services, and the temptations, of that American wilderness.

Here was Mr. Bradford, in the year 1621, unanimously chosen the governour of the plantation: the difficulties whereof were such, that if he had not been a person of more than ordinary piety, wisdom and courage, he must have sunk under them. He had, with a laudable industry, been laying up a treasure of experiences, and he had now occasion to use it: indeed, nothing but an experienced man could have been suitable to the necessities of the people. The potent nations of the Indians, into whose country they were come, would have cut them off, if the blessing of God upon his conduct had not quelled them; and if his prudence, justice and moderation had not over-ruled them, they had been ruined by their own distempers.

For two years together after the beginning of the colony, whereof he was now governour, the poor people had a great experiment of "man's not living by bread alone;" for when they were left all together without one morsel of bread for many months one after another, still the good providence of God relieved them, and supplied them, and this for the most part out of the sea. In this low condition of affairs, there was no little exercise for the prudence and patience of the governour, who chearfully bore his part in all: and, that industry might not flag, he quickly set himself to settle propriety among the new-planters; foreseeing that while the whole country laboured upon a common stock, the husbandry and business of the plantation could not flourish, as Plato and others long since dreamed that it would, if a community were established. Certainly, if the spirit which dwelt in the old Puritans, had not inspired these new-planters, they had sunk under the burden of these difficulties; but our Bradford had a double portion of that spirit.

The leader of a people in a wilderness had need be a Moses; and if a Moses had not led the people of Plymouth Colony, when this worthy person was their governour, the people had never with so much unanimity and importunity still called him to lead them. Among many instances thereof, let this one piece of self-denial be told for a memorial of him, wheresoever this History shall be considered: The patent of the colony was taken in his name, running in these terms: "To William Bradford, his heirs, associates, and assigns." But when the number of the freemen was much increased, and many new townships erected, the General Court there desired of Mr. Bradford, that he would make a surrender of the same into their hands, which he willingly and presently assented unto, and confirmed it according to their desire by his hand and seal, reserving no more for himself than was his proportion, with others, by agreement.

He was a person for study as well as action; and hence, notwithstanding the difficulties through which he passed in his youth, he attained unto a notable skill in languages: the Dutch tongue was become almost as vernacular to him as the English; the French tongue he could also manage; the Latin and the Greek he had mastered; but the Hebrew he most of all studied, "Because," he said, "he would see with his own eyes the ancient oracles of God in their native beauty." He was also well skilled in history, in antiquity, and in philosophy; and for theology he became so versed in it, that he was an irrefragable disputant against the errors, especially those of Anabaptism, which with trouble he saw rising in his colony; wherefore he wrote some significant things for the confutation of those errors. But the crown of all was his holy, prayerful, watchful, and fruitful walk with God, wherein he was very exemplary.

At length he fell into an indisposition of body, which rendred him unhealthy for a whole winter; and as the spring advanced, his health yet more declined; yet he felt himself not what he counted sick, till one day; in the night after which, the God of heaven so filled his mind with ineffable consolations, that he seemed little short of Paul, rapt up unto the unutterable entertainments of Paradise. The next morning he told his friends, "That the good Spirit of God had given him a pledge of his happiness in another world, and the first-fruits of his eternal glory;" and on the day following he died, May 9, 1657, in the 69th year of his age — lamented by all the colonies of New-England, as a common blessing and father to them all.

Life of John Winthrop

Let Greece boast of her patient Lycurgus, the lawgiver, by whom diligence, temperance, fortitude and wit were made the fashions of a therefore long-lasting and renowned commonwealth: let Rome tell of her devout Numa, the lawgiver, by whom the most famous commonwealth saw peace triumphing over extinguished war and cruel plunders; and murders giving place to the more mollifying exercises of his religion. Our New-England shall tell and boast of her Winthrop, a lawgiver as patient as Lycurgus, but not admitting any of his criminal disorders; as devout as Numa, but not liable to any of his heathenish madnesses; a governour in whom the excellencies of Christianity made a most improving addition unto the virtues, wherein even without those he would have made a parallel for the great men of Greece, or of Rome, which the pen of a Plutarch has eternized.

Our John Winthrop, born at the mansion-house of his ancestors, at Groton in Suffolk, on June 12, 1587, enjoyed afterwards an agreeable education. But though he would rather have devoted himself unto the study of Mr. John Calvin, than of Sir Edward Cook; nevertheless, the accomplishments of a lawyer were those wherewith Heaven made his chief opportunities to be serviceable.

Being made, at the unusually early age of eighteen, a justice of peace, his virtues began to fall under a more general observation; and he not only so bound himself to the behaviour of a Christian, as to become exemplary for a conformity to the laws of Christianity in his own conversation, but also discovered a more than ordinary measure of those qualities which adorn an officer of humane society. Accordingly when the noble design of carrying a colony of chosen people into an American wilderness, was by some eminent persons undertaken, this eminent person was, by the consent of all, chosen for the Moses, who must be the leader of so great an undertaking: and indeed nothing but a Mosaic spirit could have carried him through the temptations, to which either his farewel to his own land, or his travel in a strange land, must needs expose a gentleman of his education. Wherefore having sold a fair estate of six or seven hundred a year, he transported himself with the effects of it into New-England in the year 1630, where he spent it upon the service of a famous plantation, founded and formed for the seat of the most reformed Christianity: and continued there, conflicting with temptations of all sorts, as many years as the nodes of the moon take to dispatch a revolution.

Were he now to be considered only as a Christian, we might therein propose him as greatly imitable. He was a very religious man; and as he strictly kept his heart, so he kept his house, under the laws of piety; there he was every day constant in holy duties, both morning and evening, and on the Lord's days, and lectures; though he wrote not after the preacher, yet such was his attention, and such his retention in hearing, that he repeated unto his family the sermons which he had heard in the congregation. But it is chiefly as a governour that he is now to be considered. Being the governour over the considerablest part of New-England, he maintained the figure and honour of his place with the spirit of a true gentleman; but yet with such obliging condescention to the circumstances of the colony, that when a certain troublesome and malicious calumniator, well known in those times, printed his libellous nick-names upon the chief persons here, the worst nick-name he could find for the governour, was John Temperwell.

But whilst he thus did, as our New-England Nehemiah, the part of a ruler in managing the public affairs of our American Jerusalem, when there were Tobijahs and San-ballats enough to vex him, and give him the experiment of Luther's observation, *Omnis qui regit est tanquam signum, in quod omnia jacula, Satan et Mundus dirigunt*,[28] he made himself still an exacter parallel unto that governour of Israel, by doing the part of a neighbour among the distressed people of the new plantation. Indeed, for a while the governour was the Joseph, unto whom the whole body of the people repaired when their corn failed them; and he continued relieving of them with his open-handed boun-ties, as long as he had any stock to do it with; and a lively faith to see the return of the "bread after many days," and not starve in the days that were to pass till that return should be seen, carried him cheerfully through those ex-pences.

Once it was observable that, on February 5, 1630, when he was distributing the last handful of the meal in the barrel unto a poor man distressed by the "wolf at the door," at that instant they spied a ship arrived at the harbour's mouth, laden with provisions for them all. Yea, the governour sometimes made his own private purse to be the publick: not by sucking into it, but by squeezing out of it; for when the publick treasure had nothing in it, he did himself defray the charges of the publick. 'Twas his custom also to send some of his family upon errands unto the houses of the poor, about their meal time, on purpose to spy whether they wanted; and if it were found that they wanted, he would make that the opportunity of sending supplies unto them. And there was one passage of his charity that was perhaps a little unusual: in an hard and long winter, when wood was very scarce at Boston, a man gave him a private information that a needy person in the neighbourhood stole wood sometimes from his pile; where-upon the governour in a seeming anger did reply, "Does he so? I'll take a course with him; go, call that man to me; I'll

warrant you I'll cure him of stealing." When the man
came, the governour considering that if he had stolen, it
was more out of necessity than disposition, said unto him,
"Friend, it is a severe winter, and I doubt you are but
meanly provided for wood; wherefore I would have you
supply your self at my wood-pile till this cold season be
over." And he then merrily asked his friends, "Whether he
had not effectually cured this man of stealing his wood?"

One would have imagined that so good a man could have
had no enemies, if we had not had a daily and woful
experience to convince us that goodness it self will make
enemies. Yea, there were persons eminent both for figure
and for number, unto whom it was almost essential to
dislike every thing that came from him; and yet he always
maintained an amicable correspondence with them; as believing that they acted according to their judgment and
conscience, or that their eyes were held by some temptation
in the worst of all their oppositions.

Great attempts were sometimes made among the freemen
to get him left out from his place in the government upon
little pretences, lest by the too frequent choice of one man,
the government should cease to be by choice; and with a
particular aim at him, sermons were preached at the anniversary Court of election, to disswade the freemen from
chusing one man twice together. This was the reward of his
extraordinary serviceableness! But when these attempts did
succeed, as they sometimes did, his profound himility appeared in that equality of mind, wherewith he applied
himself chearfully to serve the country in whatever station
their votes had alloted for him. And one year when the
votes came to be numbered, there were found six less for
Mr. Winthrop than for another gentleman who then stood
in competition: but several other persons regularly ten-
dring their votes before the election was published, were,
upon a very frivolous objection, refused by some of the
magistrates that were afraid lest the election should at last
fall upon Mr. Winthrop: which, though it was well per-

ceived, yet such was the self-denial of this patriot, that he would not permit any notice to be taken of the injury.

Were it not for the sake of introducing the exemplary skill of this wise man, at giving soft answers, one would not chuse to relate those instances of wrath which he had sometimes to encounter with; but he was for his gentleness, his forbearance, and longanimity, a pattern so worthy to be written after, that something must here be written of it. The stormiest of all the trials that ever befel this gentleman, was in the year 1645, when he was, in title, no more than deputy-governour of the colony. If the famous Cato were forty-four times called into judgment, but as often acquitted; let it not be wondred, and if our famous Winthrop were one time so. There hapning certain seditious and mutinous practices in the town of Hingham, the deputy-governour, as legally as prudently, interposed his authority for the checking of them: whereupon there followed such an enchantment upon the minds of the deputies in the General Court, that upon a scandalous petition of the delinquents unto them, wherein a pretended invasion made upon the liberties of the people was complained of, the deputy-governour was most irregularly called forth unto an ignominious hearing before them in a vast assembly; whereto with a sagacious humilitude he consented, although he shewed them how he might have refused it. The result of that hearing was, that notwithstanding the touchy jealousie of the people about their liberties lay at the bottom of all this prosecution, yet Mr. Winthrop was publickly acquitted, and the offenders were severally fined and censured. But Mr. Winthrop then resuming the place of deputy-governour on the bench, saw cause to speak unto the root of the matter after this manner:

"I shall not now speak any thing about·the past proceedings of this Court, or the persons therein concerned. Only I bless God that I see an issue of this troublesome affair. I am well satisfied that I was publickly accused, and that I am now publickly acquitted. But though I am justified before men, yet it may be the Lord hath seen so much amiss in my

administrations, as calls me to be humbled; and indeed for
me to have been thus charged by men, is it self a matter of
humiliation, whereof I desire to make a right use before the
Lord. If Miriam's father spit in her face, she is to be
ashamed. But give me leave, before you go, to say something that may rectifie the opinions of many people, from
whence the distempers have risen that have lately prevailed
upon the body of this people. The questions that have
troubled the country have been about the authority of the
magistracy, and the liberty of the people. It is you who have
called us unto this office; but being thus called, we have our
authority from God; it is the ordinance of God, and it hath
the image of God stamped upon it; and the contempt of it
has been vindicated by God with terrible examples of his
vengence. I entreat you to consider, that when you chuse
magistrates, you take them from among your selves, 'men
subject unto like passions with your selves.' If you see our
infirmities, reflect on your own, and you will not be so
severe censurers of ours. We count him a good servant who
breaks not his covenant: the covenant between us and you,
is the oath you have taken of us, which is to this purpose,
'that we shall govern you, and judge your causes, according
to God's laws, and our own, according to our best skill.' As
for our skill, you must run the hazard of it; and if there be
an error, not in the will, but only in skill, it becomes you to
bear it. Nor would I have you to mistake in the point of
your own liberty. There is a liberty of corrupt nature,
which is affected both by men and beasts, to do what they
list; and this liberty is inconsistent with authority, impa-
tient of all restraint; by this liberty, *Sumus Omnes Deteri-
ores;*[29] 'tis the grand enemy of truth and peace, and all the
ordinances of God are bent against it. But there is a civil, a
moral, a federal liberty, which is the proper end and object
of authority; it is a liberty for that only which is just and
good; for this liberty you are to stand with the hazard of
your very lives; and whatsoever crosses it is not authority,
but a distemper whereof. This liberty is maintained in a
way of subjection to authority; and the authority set over
you will in all administrations for your good be quietly
submitted unto, by all but such as have a disposition to
shake off the yoke, and lose their true liberty, by their
murmering at the honour and power of authority."

The spell that was upon the eyes of the people being thus
dissolved, their distorted and enraged notions of things all

vanished; and the people would not afterwards entrust the helm of the weather-beaten bark in any other hands but Mr. Winthrop's until he died.

Life of John Winthrop, Jr.

The eldest son of John Winthrop, Esq., the governour of one colony, was John Winthrop, Esq., the governour of another, in therefore happy New-England, born February 12, 1605, at Groton in England. His glad father bestowed on him a liberal education at the university, first of Cambridge in England, and then of Dublin in Ireland; and because travel has been esteemed no little accomplisher of a young gentleman, he then accomplished himself by travelling into France, Holland, Flanders, Italy, Germany, and as far as Turkey it self; in which places he so improved his opportunity of conversing with all sorts of learned men, that he returned home equally a subject of much experience and of great expectation.

The son of Scipio Africanus proving a degenerate person, the people forced him to pluck off a signet-ring which he wore with his father's face engraven on it. But the son of our celebrated Governour Winthrop, was on the other side so like unto his excellent father for early wisdom and virtue, that arriving at New-England with his father's family, November 4, 1631, he was, though not above twenty-three years of age, by the unanimous choice of the people, chosen a magistrate of the colony, whereof his father was the governour. For this colony he afterwards did many services, yea, and he did them abroad as well as at home; very particularly in the year 1634, when returning for England, he was by bad weather forced into Ireland, where being invited unto the house of Sir John Clotworthy, he met with many considerable persons, by conferring with whom, the affairs of New-England were not a little promoted; but it was another colony for which the providence of Heaven intended him to be such another father, as his own honourable father had been to this.

In the year 1635, Mr. Winthrop returned unto New-England, with powers from the Lord Say and the Lord Brook to settle a plantation upon the Long River of Connecticut, and a commission to be himself the governour of that plantation. But inasmuch as many good people of the Massachuset-colony had just before this taken possession of land for a new-colony thereabouts, this courteous and peaceable gentleman gave them no molestation; but having wisely accommodated the matter with them, he sent a convenient number of men, with all necessaries, to erect a fortification at the mouth of the river, where a town, with a fort, is now distinguished by the name of Say-Brook; by which happy action, the planters further up the river had no small kindness done unto them; and the Indians, which might else have been more troublesome, were kept in awe.

The self-denying gentleman, who had imployed his commission of governour so little to the disadvantage of the infant-colony at Connecticut, was himself, ere long, by election made governour of that colony. And upon the restoration of King Charles II he willingly undertook another voyage to England, on the behalf of the people under his government, whose affairs he managed with such a successful prudence, that he obtained a royal charter for them, which incorporated the colony of New-Haven with them, and invested both colonies, now happily united, with a firm grant of priviledges, beyond those of the plantations which had been settled before them.

When the governour of Athens was a philosopher — namely, Demetrius — the commonwealth so flourished, that no less than three hundred brazen statues were afterward by the thankful people erected unto his memory. And a blessed land was New-England, when there was over part of it a governour who was not only a Christian and a gentleman, but also an eminent philosopher. Such an one was our Winthrop, whose genius and faculty for experimental philosophy was advanced in his travels abroad, by his acquaintance with many learned *virtuosi.* One effect of this disposition in him, was his being furnished with noble medicines, which he most charitably and generously gave away upon all occasions; insomuch that where-ever he came, still the diseased flocked about him, as if the healing angel of Bethesda had appeared in the place; and so many were the cures which he wrought, and the lives that he saved, that if Scanderbeg might boast of his having slain in his time two thousand men with his own hands, this worthy person might have made a far more desirable boast of his having in his time healed more than so many thousands; in which beneficence to mankind, there are of his worthy children, who to this day do follow his direction and example. But it was not unto New-England alone that the respects of this accomplished philosopher were confined. For whereas, in pursuance of the methods begun by that immortally famous advancer of learning, the most illustrious Lord Chancellour Bacon, a select company of eminent persons, usuing to meet in the lodgings of Dr. Wilkins of Wadham College in Oxford, had laid the foundation of a celebrated society, which by the year 1663, being incorporated with a royal charter, hath since been among the glories of England, yea, and of mankind; and their design was to make faithful records of all the works of nature or of art, which might come under their observation, and correct what had been false, restore what should be true, preserve what should be rare, and render the knowledge of the world, as well more perfect as more useful; and by multiplied experiments both of light and fruit, advance the empire of man over the whole visible creation; it was the honour of Mr. Winthrop to be a member of this Royal Society. And accordingly among the philosophical transactions published by Mr. Oldenburgh, there are some notable communications from this inquisitive and intelligent person, whose insight into many parts of the creation, but especially of the mineral kingdom, was beyond what had been attained by the most in many parts of America.

If one would therefore desire an exact picture of this worthy man, the description which the most sober and solid writers of the great philosophick work do give of those persons, who alone are qualified for the smiles of Heaven upon their enterprizes, would have exactly fitted him. He was a studious, humble, patient, reserved and mortified person, and one in whom the love of God was fervent, the love of man sincere: and he had herewithal a certain extension of soul, which disposed him to a generous behavior towards those who, by learning, breeding and virtue, deserve respects, though of a perswasion and profession in religion very different from his own; which was that of a reformed Protestant, and a New-English Puritan.

In the year 1643, after divers essays made in some former years, the several colonies of New-England became in fact, as well as name, United Colonies. And an instrument was formed, wherein having declared, "That we all came into these parts of America with the same end and aim — namely, to advance the glory of our Lord Jesus Christ, and enjoy the liberties of the gospel with purity and peace," — it was firmly agreed between the several jurisdictions, that there should yearly be chosen two commissioners out of each, who should meet at fit places appointed for that purpose, with full powers from the General Courts in each, to concert and conclude matters of general concernment for peace or war of the several colonies thus confederated. In pursuance of this laudable confederacy, this most meritorious governour of Connecticut colony accepted the trouble of appearing as a commissioner for that colony, with the rest met at Boston, in the year 1676, when the calamities of the Indian-war were distressing the whole country: but here falling sick of a fever, he dyed on April 5, of that year, and was honourably interred in the same tomb with his honourable father.

Life of William Phips

So obscure was the original of that memorable person, whose actions I am going to relate, that I must, in a way of writing like that of Plutarch, prepare my reader for the intended relation, by first searching the archives of antiquity for a parallel. Now, because we will not parallel him with Eumenes, who, though he were the son of a poor carrier, become a governour of mighty provinces; not with Marius, whose mean parentage did not hinder his becoming a glorious defender of his country, and seven times the chief magistrate of the chiefest city in the universe, we will decline looking any further in that hemisphere of the world, and make the "hue and cry" throughout the regions of America, the New World, which he that is becoming the subject of our history, by his nativity, belonged unto. And in America, the first that meets me is Francisco Pizarro, who, though a spurious offspring, exposed when a babe in a church-porch, at a sorry village of Navarre, and afterwards employed while he was a boy in keeping of cattel, yet, at length, stealing into America, he so thrived upon his adventures there, that upon some discoveries, which with an handful of men he had in a desperate expedition made of Peru, he obtained the King of Spain's commission for the conquest of it, and at last so incredibly enriched himself by the conquest, that he was made the first Vice-roy of Peru, and created Marquess of Anatilla.

To the latter and highest part of that story, if anything hindered his Excellency Sir William Phips from affording of a parallel, it was not the want either of design, or of courage, or of conduct in himself, but it was the fate of a premature mortality. For my reader now being satisfied that a person's being obscure in his original is not always a just prejudice to an expectation of considerable matters from him, I shall now inform him that this our Phips was born February 2, A.D. 1650, at a despicable plantation on the river of Kennebeck, and almost the furthest village of the eastern settlement of New-England. And as the father of that man which was as great a blessing as England had in the age of that man was a smith, so a gun-smith — namely, James Phips, once of Bristol — had the honour of being the father to him whom we shall presently see made by the God of Heaven as great a blessing to New-England as that country could have had, if they themselves had pleased.

His friends earnestly solicited him to settle among them in a plantation of the east; but he had an unaccountable impulse upon his mind, perswading him, as he would privately hint unto some of them, "that he was born to greater matters." To come at those "greater matters," his first contrivance was to bind himself an apprentice unto a ship carpenter for four years; in which time he became a master of the trade that once, in a vessel of more than forty thousand tuns, repaired the ruins of the earth; Noah's, I mean; he then betook himself an hundred and fifty miles further a field, even to Boston, the chief town of New-England; which being a place of the most business and resort in those parts of the world, he expected there more commodiously to pursue the *Spes Majorum et Meliorum*[30] — hopes which had inspired him. At Boston, where it was that he now learned first of all to read and write, he followed his trade for about a year; and, by a laudable deportment, so recommended himself, that he married a young gentlewoman of good repute.

Within a little while after his marriage, he indented with several persons in Boston to build them a ship at Sheeps-coat River, two or three leagues eastward of Kennebeck; where having launched the ship, he also provided a lading of lumber to bring with him, which would have been to the advantage of all concerned. But just as the ship was hardly finished, the barbarous Indians on that river broke forth into an open and cruel war upon the English; and the miserable people, surprized by so sudden a storm of blood, had no refuge from the infidels but the ship now finishing in the harbour. Whereupon he left his intended lading behind him, and, instead thereof, carried with him his old neighbours and their families, free of all charges to Boston; so the first action that he did, after he was his own man, was to save his father's house, with the rest of the neighbourhood, from ruin; but the disappointment which befel him from the loss of his other lading, plunged his affairs into greater embarrassments with such as had employed him.

But he was hitherto no more than beginning to make scaffolds for further and higher actions! He was of an enterprizing genius, and naturally disdained littleness: but his disposition for business was of the Dutch mould, where, with a little shew of wit, there is as much wisdom demonstrated, as can be shewn by any nation. His talent lay not in the airs that serve chiefly for the pleasant and sudden turns of conversation; but he might say, as Themistocles, "Though he could not play upon a fiddle, yet he knew how to make a little city become a great one." He would prudently contrive a weighty undertaking, and then patiently pursue it unto the end. He was of an inclination cutting rather like a hatchet than like a razor; he would propose very considerable matters to himself, and then so cut through them, that no difficulties could put by the edge of his resolutions. Being thus of the true temper for doing of great things, he betakes himself to the sea, the right scene for such things; and upon advice of a Spanish wreck about the Bahamas, he took a voyage thither; but with little more success than what just served him a little to furnish him for a voyage to England; whither he went in a vessel, not much unlike that which the Dutchmen stamped on their first coin, with these words about it: *Incertum quo Fata ferant*.[31] Having first informed himself that there was another Spanish wreck, wherein was lost a mighty treasure, hitherto undiscovered, he had a strong impression upon his mind that he must be the discoverer; and he made such representations of his design at White-Hall, that by the year 1683 he became the captain of a King's ship, and arrived at New-England commander of the Algier-Rose, a frigot of eighteen guns and ninety-five men.

So proper was his behaviour, that the best noblemen in the kingdom now admitted him into their conversation; but yet he was opposed by powerful enemies, that clogged his affairs with such demurrages, and such disappointments, as would have wholly discouraged his designs, if his patience had not been invincible. "He who can wait, hath what he desireth." Thus his indefatigable patience, with a proportionable diligence, at length overcame the difficulties that had been thrown in his way; and prevailing with the Duke of Albemarle, and some other persons of quality, to fit him out, he set sail for the fishing-ground, which had been so well baited half an hundred years before.

Captain Phips now coming up to London in the year 1687, with near three hundred thousand pounds sterling [from the Spanish wreck] aboard him, did acquit himself with such an exemplary honesty, that partly by his fulfilling his assurances to the seamen, and partly by his exact and punctual care to have his employers defrauded of nothing that might conscientiously belong unto them, he had less than sixteen thousand pounds left unto himself; as an acknowledgment of which honesty in him, the Duke of Albemarle made unto his wife, whom he never saw, a present of a golden cup, near a thousand pound in value. The character of an honest man he had so merited in the whole course of his life, and especially in this last act of it, that this, in conjunction with his other serviceable qualities, procured him the favours of the greatest persons in the nation. Accordingly the King, in consideration of the service done by him, in bringing such a treasure into the nation, conferred upon him the honour of knighthood; and if we now reckon him a knight of the golden fleece, the stile might pretend unto some circumstances that would justifie it. Or call him, if you please, "the knight of honesty;" for it was honesty with industry that raised him; and he became a mighty river, without the running in of muddy water to make him so. Reader, now make a pause, and behold one raised by God!

Now, the arrival of Sir William Phips to the government of New-England, was at a time when a governour would have had occasion for all the skill in sorcery that was ever necessary to a Jewish Counsellor; a time when scores of poor people had newly fallen under a prodigious possession of devils, which it was then generally thought had been by witchcrafts introduced. It is to be confessed and bewailed, that many inhabitants of New-England, and young people especially, had been led away with little sorceries, wherein they "did secretly those things that were not right against the Lord their God;" they would often cure hurts with spells, and practice detestable conjurations with sieves, and keys, and pease, and nails, and horse-shoes, and other implements, to learn the things for which they had a forbidden and impious curiosity.

The devils which had been so played withal, and, it may be, by some few criminals more explicitly engaged and imployed, now broke in upon the country, after as astonishing a manner as was ever heard of. Some scores of people, first about Salem, the centre and first-born of all the towns in the colony, and afterwards in several other places, were arrested with many preternatural vexations upon their bodies, and a variety of cruel torments, which were evidently inflicted from the daemons of the invisible world. The people that were infected and infested with such daemons, in a few days' time arrived unto such a refining alteration upon their eyes, that they could see their tormentors: they saw a devil of a little stature, and of a tawny colour, attended still with spectres that appeared in more humane circumstances.

These tormentors tendred unto the afflicted a book, requiring them to sign it, or to touch it at least, in token of their consenting to be listed in the service of the devil; which they refusing to do, the spectres under the command of that blackman, as they called him, would apply themselves to torture them with prodigious molestations.

The afflicted wretches were horribly distorted and convulsed; they were pinched black and blue: pins would be run every where in their flesh; they would be scalded until they had blisters raised on them; and a thousand other things before hundreds of witnesses were done unto them, evidently preternatural: for if it were preternatural to keep a rigid fast for nine, yea, for fifteen days together; or if it were preternatural to have one's hands tyed close together with a rope to be plainly seen, and then by unseen hands presently pulled up a great way from the earth before a croud of people; such preternatural things were endured by them.

But of all the preternatural things which befel these people, there were none more unaccountable than those wherein the prestigious daemons would ever now and then cover the most corporeal things in the world with a fascinating mist of invisibility. As now; a person was cruelly assaulted by a spectre, that, she said, run at her with a spindle, though no body else in the room could see either the spectre or the spindle: at last, in her agonies, giving a snatch at the spectre, she pulled the spindle away; and it was no sooner got into her hand, but the other folks then present beheld that it was indeed a real, proper, iron spindle; which, when they locked up very safe, it was nevertheless by the daemons taken away to do farther mischief.

Again, a person was haunted by a most abusive spectre, which came to her, she said, with a sheet about her, though seen to none but herself. After she had undergone a deal of teaze from the annoyance of the spectre, she gave a violent snatch at the sheet that was upon it; where-from she tore a corner, which in her hand immediately was beheld by all that were present, a palpable corner of a sheet: and her father, which was now holding of her, catched, that he might keep what his daughter had so strangely seized; but the spectre had like to have wrung his hand off, by endeavouring to wrest it from him; however, he still held it, and several times this odd accident was renewed in the family. There wanted not the oaths of good credible people to these particulars.

Once more: the miserable exclaimed extreamly of branding irons heating at the fire on the hearth to mark them. Now, though the standersby could see no irons, yet they could see distinctly the print of them in the ashes, and smell them too as they were carried by the not-seen furies unto the poor creatures for whom they were intended; and those poor creatures were thereupon so stigmatized with them, that they will bear the marks of them to their dying day. Nor are these the tenth part of the prodigies that fell out among the inhabitants of New-England.

Flashy people may burlesque these things, but when hundreds of the most sober people in a country where they have as much mother-wit certainly as the rest of mankind, know them to be true, nothing but the absurd and froward spirit of Sadducism can question them. I have not yet mentioned so much as one thing that will not be justified, if it be required by the oaths of more considerable persons than any that can ridicule these odd phoenomena.

But the worst part of this astonishing tragedy is yet behind; wherein Sir William Phips, at last being dropt, as it were from the machine of heaven, was an instrument of easing the distresses of the land, now "so darkened by the wrath of the Lord of Hosts." There were very worthy men upon the spot where the assault from hell was first made, who apprehended themselves called from the God of heaven to sift the business unto the bottom of it; and, indeed, the continual impressions, which the outcries and the havocks of the afflicted people that lived nigh unto them caused on their minds, gave no little edge to this apprehension.

The persons were men eminent for wisdom and virtue, and they went about their enquiry into the matter, as driven unto it by a conscience of duty to God and the world. The existence of such witches was now taken for granted by those good men, wherein so far the generality of reasonable men have thought they ran well; and they soon received the confessions of some accused persons to confirm them in it: but then they took one thing more for granted, wherein 'tis now as generally thought they went out of the way. The afflicted people vehemently accused several persons in several places that the spectres which afflicted them, did exactly resemble them; until the importunity of the accusations did provoke the magistrates to examine them. When many of the accused came upon their examination, it was found that the daemons then a thousand ways abusing of the poor afflicted people, had with a marvellous exactness represented them; yea, it was found, that many of the accused, but casting their eye on the afflicted, the afflicted, though their faces were never so much another way, would fall down and lye in a sort of a swoon, wherein they would continue, whatever hands were laid upon them, until the hands of the accused came to touch them, and then they would revive immediately; and it was found, that various kinds of natural actions, done by many of the accused in or to their own bodies, as leaning, bending, turning awry, or squeezing their hands, or the like, were presently attended with the like things preternaturally done upon the bodies of the afflicted, though they were so far asunder, that the afflicted could not at all observe the accused.

It was also found, that the flesh of the afflicted was often bitten at such a rate, that not only the print of teeth would be left on their flesh, but the very slaver of spittle too; and there would appear just such a set of teeth as was in the accused, even such as might be clearly distinguished from other peoples. And usually the afflicted went through a terrible deal of seeming difficulties from the tormenting spectres, and must be long waited on before they could get a breathing space from their torments to give in their testimonies.

Now, many good men took up an opinion, that the providence of God would not permit an innocent person to come under such a spectral representation; and that a concurrence of so many circumstances would prove an accused person to be in a confederacy with the daemons thus afflicting of the neighbours; they judged that, except these things might amount unto a conviction, it would scarce be possible ever to convict a witch: and they had some philosophical schemes of witchcraft, and of the method and manner wherein magical poisons operate, which further supported them in their opinion.

Sundry of the accused persons were brought unto their trial, while this opinion was yet prevailing in the minds of the judges and the juries, and perhaps the most of the people in the country, then mostly suffering; and though against some of them that were tried there came in so much other evidence of their diabolical compacts, that some of the most judicious, and yet vehement opposers of the notions then in vogue, publickly declared, "Had they themselves been on the bench, they could not have acquitted them;" nevertheless, divers were condemned, against whom the chief evidence was founded in the spectral exhibitions.

On the other part, there were many persons of great judgment, piety and experience, who from the beginning were very much dissatisfied at these proceedings; they feared lest the devil would get so far into the faith of the people, that for the sake of many truths which they might find him telling of them, they would come at length to believe all his lies; whereupon what a desolation of names — yea, and of lives also — would ensue, a man might, without much witchcraft, be able to prognosticate; and they feared, lest in such an extraordinary descent of wicked spirits from their high places upon us, there might such principles be taken up, as, when put into practice, would unavoidably cause the righteous to perish with the wicked, and procure the blood-shed of persons like the Gibeonites, whom some learned men suppose to be under a false pretence of witchcraft, by Saul exterminated.

In fine, the country was in a dreadful ferment, and wise men foresaw a long train of dismal and bloody consequences. Hereupon they first advised that the afflicted might be kept asunder in the closest privacy; and one particular person, (whom I have cause to know,) in pursuance of this advice, offered himself singly to provide accommodations for any six of them, that so the success of more than ordinary prayer with fasting might, with patience, be experienced, before any other courses were taken.

And Sir William Phips arriving to his government, after this ensnarling horrible storm was begun, did consult the neighbouring ministers of the province. Now, upon a deliberate review of these things, his Excellency first reprieved, and then pardoned many of them that had been condemned; and there fell out several strange things that caused the spirit of the country to run as vehemently upon the acquitting of all the accused, as it by mistake ran at first upon the condemning of them. Some that had been zealously of the mind, that the devils could not in the shapes of good men afflict other men, were terribly confuted, by having their own shapes, and the shapes of their most intimate and valued friends, thus abused.

Sir William Phips now beheld such daemons hideously scattering fire about the country, in the exasperations which the minds of men were on these things rising unto; and therefore when he had well canvased a cause, which perhaps might have puzzled the wisdom of the wisest men on earth to have managed, without any error in their administrations, he thought, if it would be any error at all, it would certainly be the safest for him to put a stop unto all future prosecutions, as far as it lay in him to do it.

He did so, and for it he had not only the printed acknowledgments of the New-Englanders, who publickly thanked him, "As one of the tribe of Zebulun, raised up from among themselves, and spirited as well as commissioned to be the steers-man of a vessel befogged in the *mare mortuum* of witchcraft, who now so happily steered her course, that she escaped shipwreck, and was safely again moored under the Cape of Good Hope; and cut asunder the Circaean knot of enchantment, more difficult to be dissolved than the famous Gordian one of old."

Book III

POLYBIUS: NEW ENGLAND DIVINES

Life of John Cotton

Were I master of the pen wherewith Palladius embalmed his Chrysostom, the Greek patriark, or Posidonius eternized his Austin, the Latin oracle, among the ancients; or, were I owner of the quill wherewith, among the moderns, Beza celebrated his immortal Calvin, or Fabius immortalized his venerable Beza; the merits of John Cotton would oblige me to employ it, in the preserving his famous memory. If Boston be the chief seat of New-England, it was Cotton that was the father and glory of Boston: upon which account it becomes a piece of pure justice, that the life of him, who above all men gave life to his country, should bear no little figure in its intended history.

The religious parents of Mr. Cotton were solicitous to have him indued with a learned as well as a pious education; and being neither so rich, that the *Mater Artis* could have no room to do her part, nor so poor that the *Res angusta domi*[32] should clog his progress, they were well fitted thereby to bestow such an education upon him. His first instruction was under a good school-master, one Mr. Johnson, in the town of Derby; whereon the intellectual endowments of all sorts, with which the God of our spirits adorned him, so discovered themselves, that, at the age of thirteen, his proficiency procured him admission into Trinity-College in Cambridge.

Upon the desires of Emanuel-College, Mr. Cotton was not only removed unto that college, but also preferred unto a fellowship in it; in order whereunto, he did, according to the critical and laudable statutes of the house, go through a very severe examen of his fitness for such a station; wherein 'twas particularly remarked, that the poser trying his Hebrew skill by the third chapter of Isaiah, a chapter which, containing more hard words than any one paragraph of the Bible, might therefore have puzzled a very good Herbrician, yet he made nothing of it. He was afterwards the head lecturer, the dean, the catechist, in that famous college; and became a tutor to many scholars, who afterwards proved famous persons, and had cause to bless God for the faithful, and ingenious, and laborious communicativeness of this their tutor.

Hitherto we have seen the life of Mr. Cotton, while he was not yet alive! Though the restraining and preventing grace of God had kept him from such outbreakings of sin as defile the lives of most in the world, yet, like the old man who for such a cause ordered this epitaph to be written on his grave, "Here lies an old man, who lived but seven years," he reckoned himself to have been but a dead man, as being "alienated from the life of God," until he had experienced that regeneration in his own soul, which was thus accomplished. The Holy Spirit of God had been at work upon his young heart, by the ministry of that reverend and renowned preacher of righteousness, Mr. Perkins; but he resisted and smothered those convictions, through a vain perswasion that, if he became a godly man, 'twould spoil him for being a learned one. But he was, at length, more effectually awakened by a sermon of Dr. Sibs, wherein was discoursed the misery of those who had only a negative righteousness, or a civil, sober, honest blamelessness before men. Mr. Cotton became now very sensible of his own miserable condition before God; and the arrows of these convictions did stick so fast upon him, that after no less than three year's disconsolate apprehensions under them, the grace of God made him a thoroughly renewed Christian, and filled him with a sacred joy, which accompanied him unto the fulness of joy for ever.

The well-disposed people of Boston in Lincolnshire invited Mr. Cotton to become their minister; with which
invitation, out of a sincere and serious desire to serve our
Lord in his gospel, after the solemnest addresses to heaven
for guidance in such a solemn affair, he complied. About
half a year after Mr. Cotton had been at Boston, thus
usefully employed, he visited Cambridge, that he might
then and there proceed batchellor of divinity, which he
did. After he had been three years in Boston, his careful
studies and prayers brought him to apprehend more of evil
remaining unreformed in the Church of England than he
had heretofore considered; and from this time he became a
conscientious non-conformist, unto the unscriptural ceremonies and constitutions yet maintained by that church;
but such was his interest in the hearts of the people, that
his non-conformity, instead of being disturbed, was indeed
embraced by the greatest part of the town. However, at last,
complaints being made against him unto the Bishop's
courts, he was for a while then put under the circumstances
of a silenced minister; in all which while, he would still
give his presence at the publick sermons, though never at
the common prayers of the conformable. He was now
offered, not only the liberty of his ministry, but very great
preferment in it also, if he would but conform to the
scrupled rites, though but in one act, and but for one time;
nevertheless, his tender soul, afraid of being thereby pol-
luted, could not in the least comply with such temptations.
A storm of many troubles upon him was now gathering;
but it was very strangely diverted! For that very man who
had occasioned this affliction to him, now became heartily
afflicted for his own sin in doing of it; and a stedfast,
constant, prudent friend; presenting a pair of gloves to a
proctor of an higher court, then appealed unto that proctor
without Mr. Cotton's knowledge, swore, *In Animam Domi-
ni*,[33] that Mr. Cotton was a conformable man; which
things issued in Mr. Cotton's being restored unto the exercise of his ministry.

The good spirit of God, so plentifully and powerfully accompanied the ministry of this excellent man, that a great reformation was thereby wrought in the town of Boston. Profaneness was extinguished, superstition was abandoned, religion was embraced and practised among the body of the people; yea, the mayor, with most of the magistrates, were now called Puritans, and the Satanical party was become insignificant. As to the matter of non-conformity, Mr. Cotton was come to forbear the ceremonies enjoyned in the Church of England.

But this was not all: for Mr. Cotton was also come to believe, that Scripture bishops were appointed to rule no larger a diocess than a particular congregation; and that the ministers of the Lord, with the keys of ecclesiastical government, are given by him to a congregational church. It hence came to pass, that our Lord Jesus Christ was now worshipped in Boston, without the use of the liturgy, or of those vestments, which are by Zanchy called *Execrabiles Vestes*,[34] yea, the sign of the cross was laid aside, not only in baptism, but also in the mayor's mace, as worthy to be made a Nehushtan, because it had been so much abused unto idolatry. And besides all this, there were some scores of pious people in the town, who more exactly formed themselves into an evangelical church-state, by entring into covenant with God, and with one another, "to follow after the Lord, in the purity of his worship." However, the main bent and aim of Mr. Cotton's ministry was, "to preach a crucified Christ;" and the inhabitants of Boston observed, that God blessed them in their secular concernments, re-markably the more, through his dwelling among them; for many strangers, and some, too, that were gentlemen of good quality, resorted unto Boston, and some removed their habitations thither on his account; whereby the prosperity of the place was very much promoted.

Although our Lord hath hitherto made the discretion and vigilancy of Mr. Thomas Leveret (afterwards a doubly honoured elder of the church, in another land) the happy occasion of diverting many designs to molest Mr. Cotton for his non-conformity, yet when the sins of the place had ripened it for so dark a vengeance of heaven as the removing of this eminent light, a storm of persecution could no longer be avoided. A debauched fellow in the town, who had been punished by the magistrates for his debaucheries, contrived and resolved a revenge upon them, for their justice: and having no more effectual way to vent the cursed malice of his heart, than by bringing them into trouble at the High Commission Court, up he goes to London, with informations to that court, that the magistrates did not kneel at the sacrament, nor observe some other ceremonies by law imposed. When some that belonged unto the court signified unto this informer that he must put in the minister's name: "Nay," (said he) "the minister is an honest man, and never did me any wrong:" but it being farther pressed upon him, that all his complaints would be insignificant, if the minister's name were not in them, he then did put it in: and letters missive were dispatched incontinently, to convent Mr. Cotton before the infamous High Commission Court.

Mr. Cotton, therefore, now, with supplications unto the God of Heaven for his direction, joined consultations of good men on earth; and among others, he did, with some of his Boston friends, visit old Mr. Dod, unto whom he laid open the difficult case now before him, without any intimation of his own inclination, whereby the advice of that holy man might have been at all forestalled. Mr. Dod, upon the whole, said thus unto him: "I am old Peter, and therefore must stand still, and bear the brunt; but you, being young Peter, may go whether you will, and ought, being persecuted in one city, to flee unto another." And when the Boston friends urged, "that they would support and protect Mr. Cotton, though privately; and that if he should leave them, very many of them would be exposed unto extreme temptation:" he readily answered, "That the removing of a minister was like the draining of a fish pond: the good fish will follow the water, but eels, and other baggage fish, will stick in the mud." Which things, when Mr. Cotton heard, he was not a little confirmed in his inclination to leave the land.

Cotton being now at London, there were three places which offered themselves to him for his retreat; Holland, Barbadoes, and New-England. As for Holland, the character and condition which famous Mr. Hooker had reported thereof, took off his intentions of removing thither. And Barbadoes had not near such encouraging circumstances, upon the best accounts, as New-England; where our Lord Jesus Christ had a more than ordinary thing to be done for his glory, in an American wilderness, and so would send over a more than ordinary man, to be employed in the doing of it. Thither, even to that religious and reformed plantation, after the solemnest applications to Heaven for direction, this great person bent his resolutions: and letters procured from the church of Boston, by Mr. Winthrop, the governour of the colony, had their influence on the matter.

"The churches now had rest, and were edified: and there were daily added unto the churches those that were to be saved." Now, though the poor people were fed with "the bread of adversity, and the waters of affliction," yet they counted themselves abundantly compensated by this, that "their eyes might see such teachers" as were now to be seen among them. The faith and the order in the churches was generally glorious, whatever little popular confusions, might in some few places eclipse the glory. But the warm sunshine will produce a swarm of insects; whilst matters were going on thus prosperously, the cunning and malice of Satan, to break the prosperity of the churches, brought in a generation of hypocrites, who "crept in unawares, turning the grace of our God into lasciviousness." A company of Antinomian and Familistical sectaries were strangely crouded in among our more orthodox planters; by the artifices of which busie opinionists there was a dangerous blow given, first unto the faith, and so unto the peace of the churches. In the storm thus raised, it is incredible what obloquy came to be cast upon Mr. Cotton, as if he had been the patron of these destroyers; merely because they, willing to have a "great person in admiration, because of advantage," falsly used the name of this "great person," by the credit thereof to disseminate and dissemble their errors; and because the chief of them, in their private conferences with him, would make such fallacious profession of gospel-truths, that his Christian and abused charity would not permit him to be so hasty as many others were in censuring of them.

However, the report given of Mr. Cotton on this occasion, by one Baily, a Scotchman, in a most scandalous pamphlet, called, "A Disswasive," written to cast an odium on the churches of New-England, by vilifying him, that was one of their most eminent servants, are most horrid injuries; for there being upon the encouragement of the success which the old Nicene, Constantinopolitan, Ephesine, and Chalcedonian councils had, in the extinguishing of several successive heresies, a council now called at Cambridge, Mr. Cotton, after some debates with the reverend assembly, upon some controverted points of justification, most vigorously joined with the other ministers of the country in testifying against the hateful doctrines, whereby the churches has been troubled.

'Tis true, such was Mr. Cotton's holy ingenuity, that when he perceived the advantage which erroneous and heretical persons in his church had from his abused charity taken to spread their dangerous opinions, before he was aware of them, he did publickly sometimes with tears bewail it, "That the enemy had sown so many tares whilst he had been asleep." Nevertheless, 'tis as true, that nothing ever could be baser than the disingenuity of those pamphleteers, who took advantage hence to catch these tears in their venemous ink horns, and employ them for so many blots upon the memory of a righteous man, "worthy to be had in everlasting remembrance."

These clouds being thus happily blown over, the rest of his days were spent in a more settled peace; and Mr. Cotton's growing and spreading fame, like Joseph's bough, "ran over the wall" of the Atlantic ocean, unto such a degree, that in the year 1641 some great persons in England were intending to have sent over a ship on purpose to fetch him over, for the sake of the service that such a man as he might then do to the church of God, then travelling in the nation. But although their doubt of his willingness to remove caused them to forbear that method of obtaining him, yet the principal members in both houses of parliament wrote unto him, with an opportunity for his return into England; which had prevailed with him, if the dismal showers of blood, quickly after breaking upon the nation, had not made such afflictive impressions upon him as to prevent his purpose. He continued therefore in Boston unto his dying day; counting it a great favour of Heaven unto him, that he was delivered from "the unsettledness of habitation," which was not among the least of the calamities that exercised the apostles of our Lord. Nineteen years and odd months he spent in this place, doing of good publickly and privately, unto all sorts of men, as it became "a good man full of faith, and of the Holy Ghost."

Life of John Davenport

Mr. John Davenport was born at Coventry, in the year 1597, of worthy parents; a father who was mayor of the city, and a pious mother, who, having lived just long enough to devote him, as Hannah did, her Samuel, unto the service of the sanctuary, left him under the more immediate care of Heaven to fit him for that service. The grace of God sanctified him with good principles, while he had not yet seen two sevens of years in an evil world; and by that age he had also made such attainments in learning, as to be admitted into Brasen-Nose Colledge, in Oxford. From thence, when he was but nineteen years old, he was called unto publick and constant preaching in the city of London, as an assistant unto another divine; where his notable accomplishments for a minister, and his couragious residence with, and visiting of his flock, in a dreadful plague-time, caused much notice to be quickly taken of him. His degree of master of arts he took not, until, in course, he was to proceed batchellor of divinity: and then with universal approbation, he received both of these laurels together.

About the year 1626, there were several eminent persons, among whom were two doctors of divinity, with two other divines, and four lawyers, whereof one the King's Serjeant at law, and four citizens, whereof one the Lord Mayor of London, engaged in a design to procure a purchase of impropriations, and with the profits thereof to maintain a constant, able, and painful ministry in those parts of the kingdom where there was most want of such a ministry. The divines concerned in this design, were Dr. Gouge, Dr. Sibs, Mr. Offspring, and our Mr. Davenport; and such an incredible progress was made in it, that it is judged all the impropriations in England would have been honestly and easily recovered unto the immediate service of the reformed religion. But Bishop Laud, looking with a jealous eye on this undertaking, least it might in time give a secret growth to non-conformity, he obtained a bill to be exhibited in the Exchequer Chamber, by the King's Attorney-General, against the feoffees that had the management of it.

The issue of the business was this: the court condemned their proceedings as dangerous to the church and state; pronouncing the gifts, feoffments, and contrivances, made to the uses aforesaid, to be illegal, and so dissolved the same, confiscating their money unto the King's use. Yet the criminal part referred unto, was never prosecuted in the star-chamber; because the design was generally approved, and multitudes of discreet and devout men extreamly resented the ruine of it.

It happened that soon after this, the famous Mr. John Cotton was fallen under such a storm of persecution for his non-conformity, as made it necessary for him to propose and purpose a removal out of the land; whereupon Mr. Davenport, with several other great and good men, considering the eminent learning, prudence, and holiness of that excellent person, could be at no rest until they had by a solemn conference informed themselves of what might move him to such a resolution. The issue of the conference was, that instead of their disswading him from exposing himself to such sufferings as were now before him, he convinced them of the truth in the cause for which he suffered; and they became satisfied both of the evil in sundry matters of worship and order imposed upon them, and of the duty which lay upon them, in their places to endeavour the reformation of things in the church, according to the word of God. Mr. Davenport's inclination to non-conformity, from this time, fell under the' notice and anger of his diocesan; who presently determined the marks of his vengeance for him: of which being seasonably and sufficiently advertised, he convened the principal persons under his pastoral charge in Coleman-street, at a general vestry, desiring them on this occasion to declare what they would advise; for acknowledging the right which they had in him as their pastor, he would not by any danger be driven from any service which they should expect or demand at his hands; but he would imitate the example of Luther, who, upon letters from the church at Wittenberg, from whence he had withdrawn for his security, upon the direction of the Duke of Saxony, returned unto the couragious exercise of his ministry. Upon a serious deliberation, they discharged his conscientious obligation, by agreeing with him that it would be best for him to resign; but although he now hoped for something of a quiet life, his hope was disappointed; for he was continually dogged by raging busie pursuivants, from whom he had no safety but by retiring into Holland.

Over to Holland he went, in the latter end of the year 1633, where the messengers of the church, under the charge of Mr. Paget, met him in his way to Amsterdam, inviting

him to become the colleague of their aged pastor. But Mr.
Davenport had not been long there, before his indisposition
to the promiscuous baptising of children, concerning whom
there was no charitable or tolerable testimony of their
belonging to Christian parents, was by Mr. Paget so improved against him, as to procure him the displeasure of
the Dutch classes in the neighbourhood. But the upshot of
all was, that he returned back to London; where he told his
friends, "That he thought God carried him over into Holland, on purpose to bear witness against that promiscuous
baptism, which at least bordered very near upon a profana-
tion of the holy institution."

He observed, that when a reformation of the church has
been brought about in any part of the world, it has rarely
been afterwards carried on any one step further than the
first reformers did succeed in their first endeavours; he
observed that as easily might the ark have been removed
from the mountains of Ararat, where it first grounded, as a
people get any ground in reformation, after and beyond the
first remove of the reformers. And this observation quick-
ned him to embark in a design of reformation, wherein he
might have opportunity to drive things in the first essay, as
near to the precept and pattern of Scripture, as they could
be driven. The plantation of New-England afforded him
this opportunity, with the chief undertakers whereof he
had many consultations, before he had ever taken up any
purpose of going himself into that part of the world; and
he had, indeed, a very great stroke in the encouraging and
enlivening of that noble undertaking.

And while he was in Holland, he received letters of Mr.
Cotton from the country whereto he had thus been a
father; telling him, "That the order of the churches and
the commonwealth was now so settled in New-England, by
common consent, that it brought into his mind the new
heaven and the new earth, wherein dwells righteousness."
Wherefore, soon after his return for London, he shipped
himself, with several eminent Christians, and their families,

for New-England; where, by the good hand of God upon them, they arrived in the summer of the year 1637.

Mr. Cotton welcomed Mr. Davenport, as Moses did Jethro, hoping that he would be "as eyes unto them in the wilderness." For by the cunning and malice of Satan, all things in this New-English wilderness were then surprised into a deal of confusion, on the occasion of the Antinomian opinions then spread abroad; but the learning and wisdom of this worthy man in the synod then assembled at Cambridge, did contribute more than a little to dispel the fascinating mists which had suddenly disordered all our affairs. Having done his part in that blessed work, he, with his friends, who were more fit for Zebulon's ports than for Issachar's tents, chose to go farther westward; where they began a plantation and a colony, since distinguished by the name of New-Haven; and endeavoured, according to his understanding, a yet stricter conformity to the word of God, in settling of all matters, both civil and sacred, than he had yet seen exemplified in any other part of the world. There the famous church of New-Haven, as well as the other neighbouring towns, enjoyed his ministry, his discipline, his government, and his universal direction for many years together: even till after the restoration of King Charles II Connecticut and New-Haven were by one charter incorporated.

It is a notable expression, and a wonderful concession of that great Cardinal Bellermine, the last Goliah of the Romish Philistines: "The church" (he says) "intentionally gathers only true believers, and if she knew who were wicked and faithless, either she would not admit them at all, or, if they were accidentally admitted, she would exclude them." Our Davenport, conceiving it a shame that any Protestant should protest for less church purity than what the confessions of a learned Papist allowed, ere he was aware, to be contended for, did now at New-Haven make church purity to be one of his greatest concernments and endeavours. It was his declared principle, that more is required of men, in order to their being members of an instituted church, than that they profess the Christian faith, and ask the visible seals of the covenant in the fellowship of the church; all which may be done by persons notoriously scandalous in their lives, from whom the command is, "turn away;" but ony such persons may be received as members of a particular church, who (according to Matt. XVI 18, 19) make such a publick profession of their faith, as the church may, in charitable discretion, judge has blessedness annexed unto it, and such as flech and blood hath not revealed. In pursuance of this principle, he was, like his dear friend, that great man, Dr. Thomas Goodwin, perswaded, "that (as he speaks) there are many rules in the word, whereby it is meet for us to judge who are saints; by which rules those who are betrusted to receive men unto ordinances in churches, are to be guided, and so to separate between the precious and the unclean, as the priests of old were enabled and commanded by ceremonial differences, which God then made to typifie the like discrimination of persons." And, therefore, making the marks of a repenting and a believing soul, given in the word of God, the rules of his tryals, he used a more than ordinary exactness in trying those that were admitted unto the communion of the church: indeed, so very thoroughly, and, I had almost said, severely strict, were the terms of his communion, and so much, I had well nigh said, overmuch, were the golden snuffers of the sanctuary employed by him in his exercise of discipline towards those that were admitted, that he did all that was possible to render the renowned church of New-Haven like the New-Jerusalem; and yet, after all, the Lord gave him to see that in this world it was impossible to see a church state, whereinto there "enters nothing which defiles." This great man hath himself, in one of his own treatises, observed it: "The officers and brethren of the church are but men, who judge by the outward appearance. Therefore their judgment is fallible, and hath deceived."

After this, the remaining days of this eminent person were worn away under the unhappy temptations of a wilderness. It so happened that the most part of the first church in Boston, the metropolis of the colony, out of respect unto his vast abilities, had applied themselves unto him, to succeed those famous lights, Cotton, and Norton, and Wilson, who having from that "golden candlestick" illuminated the whole country, were now gone to shine in an higher orb. His removal from New-Haven was clogged with many temptatious difficulties, but he broke through them all, in expectation to do what he judged would be a more comprehensive service unto the churches of New-England, than could have been done by him in his now undistinguished colony. But his removal did seem too much to verifie an observation, by the famous Dr. Tuckney thus expressed; "It is ill transplanting a tree that thrives in the soil;" for accepting the call of Boston-Church, in the year 1667, that church, and the world, must enjoy him no longer than till the year 1670; when on March 15, aged seventy two years, he was by apoplexy fetched away to that glorious world, where the spirits of Cotton and Davenport are together in heaven, as their bodies are now in one tomb on earth.

To conclude: there will be but an unjust account given of the things preached and written by this reverend man, if we do not mention one singular favour of Heaven unto him. It is well known that, in the earliest of the primitive times, the faithful did, in a literal sense, believe the "second coming" of the Lord Jesus Christ, and the rising and reigning of the saints with him, a thousand years before the "rest of the dead live again;" a doctrine which, however, some of later years have counted it heretical; yet, in the days of Irenaeus, was questioned by none but such as were counted hereticks. 'Tis evident, from Justin Martyr, that this doctrine of the Chiliad was in his days embraced among all orthodox Christians; nor did this kingdom of our Lord begin to be doubted until the kingdom of antichrist began to advance into a considerable figure; and then it fell chiefly under the reproaches of such men as were fain to deny the divine authority of the book of Revelation, and of the second Epistle of Peter.

So the mystery of our Lord's "appearing in his kingdom," lay buried in Popish darkness, till the light thereof had a fresh dawn, since the antichrist entred into the last half time of the period allotted for him; and now, within the last few sevens of years, as things grow nearer to accomplishment, learned and pious men, in great numbers every where, come to receive, explain, and maintain the old faith about it. But here was the special favour of Heaven to our Davenport, that so many years ago, when in both Englands the true notion of the Chiliad was hardly apprehended by as many divines of note as there are mouths of Nilus, yet this worthy man clearly saw into it, and both preached and wrote those very things about the future state, and coming of the Lord, the calling of the Jews, and the first and second resurrection of the dead, which do now of late years get more ground against the opposition of the otherwise minded, and find a kinder entertainment among them that "search the Scriptures:" and whereof he afterwards, when he was an old man, gave the world a little taste, in a judicious preface before a most learned and nervous treatise, composed by one that was then a young man, about "the mystery of the salvation of Israel." Even, then, so long ago it was, that he asserted, "A personal, visible, powerful, and glorious coming of the Lord Jesus Christ unto judgment, long before the end of the world."

Life of Thomas Hooker

When Toxaris met with his countryman Anacharsis in Athens, he gave him this invitation, "Come along with me, and I will shew thee at once all the wonders of Greece:" whereupon he shewed him Solon, as the person in whom here centered all the glories of that city or country. I shall now invite my reader to behold at once the "wonders" of New-England, and it is in one Thomas Hooker that he shall behold them.

This our Hooker, was born at Marfield, in Leicestershire, about the year 1586, of parents that were neither unable nor unwilling to bestow upon him a liberal education; whereto the early and lively sparkles of wit observed in him did very much encourage them. His natural temper was cheerful and courteous; but it was accompanied with such a sensible grandeur of mind, as caused his friends, without the help of astrology, to prognosticate that he was born to be considerable. The influence which he had upon the reformation of some growing abuses, when he was one of the proctors in the university, was a thing that more eminently signalized him, when his more publick appearance in the world was coming on: which was attended with an advancement unto a fellowship in Emanuel Colledge, in Cambridge; the students whereof were originally designed for the study of divinity.

With what ability and fidelity he acquitted himself in his fellowship, it was a thing sensible unto the whole university. And it was while he was in this employment that the more effectual grace of God gave him the experience of a true regeneration. Mr. Hooker being now well got through the storm of soul, which had helped him unto a most experimental acquaintance with the truths of the gospel, and the way of employing and applying those truths, he was willing to serve the Church of God in the ministry, whereto he was devoted.

At his first leaving of the university, he sojourned in the house of Mr. Drake, a gentleman of great note, not far from London; whose worthy consort being visited with such distresses of soul as Mr. Hooker himself had passed through, it proved an unspeakable advantage unto both of them that he had that opportunity of being serviceable; for indeed he now had no superiour, and scarce any equal, for the skill of treating a troubled soul. When he left Mr Drake's family, he did more publickly and frequently preach about London; and in a little time he grew famous for his ministerial abilities, but especially for his notable faculty at the wise and fit management of wounded spirits. Accordingly, Chelmsford in Essex, a town of great concourse, wanting one to "break the bread of life" unto them, and hearing the fame of Mr. Hooker's powerful ministry, addressed him to become their lecturer; and he accepted their offer about the year 1626, becoming not only their lecturer, but also on the Lord's days an assistant unto one Mr. Mitchel, the incumbent of the place, who, though he were a smaller, yet being a godly person, gladly encouraged Mr. Hooker, and lived with him in a most comfortable amity.

The joy of the people in this light was "but for a season." The conscientious non-conformity of Mr. Hooker to some rites of the church of England, then vigorously pressed, especially upon such able and useful ministers as were most likely to be laid aside by their scrupling of those rites, made it necessary for him to lay down his ministry in Chelmsford, when he had been about four years there employed in it. Hereupon, at the request of several eminent persons, he kept a school in his own hired house.

While he continued thus in the heart of Essex, and in the hearts of the people there, he signalized his usefulness in many other instances. The godly ministers round about the country would have recourse unto him, to be directed and resolved in their difficult cases; and it was by his means that those godly ministers held their monthly meetings, for fasting and prayer, and profitable conferences. 'Twas the effect of his consultations, also, that such godly ministers came to be here and there settled in several parts of the country; and many others came to be better established in some great points of Christianity, by being in his neigh-

bourhood and acquaintance. He was indeed a general blessing to the church of God! But that which hindred his
taking his degree of batchellor in divinity, must also, it
seems, hinder his being a preacher of divinity; namely, his
being a non-conformist unto some things, whereof true
divinity could not approve.

The spiritual court sitting at Chelmsford, about the year
1630, had not only silenced Mr. Hooker, but also bound
him over in a bond of fifty pound to appear before the high
commission, which he could not now attend, because of an
ague then upon him. One of his hearers was bound in that
sum for his appearance; but as Paul was advised by his
friends that he would not venture into the theatre at Ephesus,
thus Mr. Hooker's friends advised him to forfeit his
bonds, rather than to throw him self any further into the
hands of his enemies. Wherefore, when the day for his
appearance came, his honest surety being reimbursed by
several good people in and near Chelmsford, sent in the for-
feited sum into the court; and Mr. Hooker having, by
the Earl of Warwick, a courteous and private recess provided for his family at a place called Old Park, he went
over to Holland.

Arriving in Holland, he was invited unto a settlement
with old Mr. Paget; but the old man being secretly willing
that Mr. Hooker should not accept of this invitation, he
contrived many ways to render him suspected unto the
classis on a suspicion that he favoured the Brownists; unto
whom he had, indeed, an extream aversion. The misunder-
standings operated so far as to occasion Mr. Hooker's removal from Amsterdam. Going from Amsterdam, he went
unto Delft; where he was most kindly received by Mr.
Forbs, an aged and holy Scotch minister, under whose
ministry many English merchants were then settled. At the
end of two years, he had a call to Rotterdam; which he the
more heartily and readily accepted, because it renewed his
acquaintance with his invaluable Dr. Ames, who had newly

left his place in the Frisian University. With him he spent
the residue of his time in Holland, and assisted him in
composing some of his discourses.

Wherefore, about this time, understanding that many of
his friends in Essex were upon the wing for a wilderness in
America, where they hoped for an opportunity to enjoy
and practice the pure worship of the Lord Jesus Christ, in
churches gathered according to his direction, he readily
answered their invitation to accompany them in this undertaking. Mr. Hooker and Mr. Cotton were, for their different
genius, the Luther and Melancthon of New-England; at
their arrival unto which country, Mr. Cotton settled with
the church of Boston, but Mr. Hooker with the church of
New-Town, having Mr. Stone for his assistant. But such
multitudes flocked over to New-England after them, that
the plantation of New-Town became too straight for them.

Accordingly, in the month of June, 1636, they removed
an hundred miles to the westward, with a purpose to settle
upon the delightful banks of Connecticut River: and there
were about an hundred persons in the first company that
made this removal; who not being able to walk above ten
miles a day, took up near a fortnight in the journey; having
no pillows to take their nightly rest upon, but such as their
father Jacob found in the way to Padan-Aram. Here Mr.
Hooker was the chief instrument of beginning another
colony, as Mr. Cotton, whom he left behind him, was of
preserving and perfecting that colony where he left him;
for, indeed, each of them were the oracle of their several
colonies.

It was his opinion that there were two great reserves of
enquiry for this age of the world; the first, wherein the
spiritual rule of our Lord's kingdom does consist, and after
what manner it is internally revealed, managed and
maintained in the souls of his people? The second, after
what order the government of our Lord's kingdom is to be
externally managed and maintained in his churches? Accordingly, having done his part for delivering the former

subject from pharisaical formality; on the one hand, and from familistical enthusiasm on the other, he was, by the solicitous importunity of his friends, prevailed withal to compose a treatise on the other subject also. Upon this occasion, he wrote his excellent book, which is entituled, "A Survey of Church Discipline;" wherein having, in the name of the other ministers in the country, as well as his own, professed his concurrence with holy and learned Mr. Rutherford, as to the number and nature of church-officers; the right of people to call their own officers; the unfitness of scandalous persons to be members of a visible church; the unwarrantableness of separation from churches for certain defective circumstances; the lawfulness, yea, needfulness of a consociation among churches; and calling in the help of such consociations, upon emerging difficulties; and the power of such consociations to proceed against a particular church, pertinaciously offending with a sentence of non-communion; he then proceeds to consider a church congregational compleatly constituted with all its officers, having full power in its self to exercise all church discipline, in all the censures thereof; and the interest which the consent of the people is to have in the exercise of this discipline.

In his administration of church discipline there were several things as imitable as observable. As he was an hearty friend unto the consociation of churches — and hence all the time that he lived, the pastors of the neighbouring churches held their frequent meetings for mutual consultation in things of common concernment — so, in his one particular church, he was very careful to have every thing done with a Christian moderation and unanimity. Wherefore he would have nothing publickly propounded unto the brethren of the church, but what had been first privately prepared by the elders; and if he feared the happening of any debate, his way aforehand was, to visit some of the more noted and leading brethren, and having engaged them to second what he should move unto the church, he rarely missed of a full concurrence: to which purpose he would say, "The elders must have a church in a church, if they would preserve the peace of the church:" and he would say, "The debating matters of difference, first before the whole body of the church, will doubtless break any church in pieces, and deliver it up unto loathsome contempt." But if any difficult or divided agitation was raised in the church, about any matter offered, he would ever put a stop to that publick agitation, by delaying the vote until another meeting; before which time, he would ordinarily, by private conferences, gain over such as were unsatisfied. As for the admission of communicants unto the Lord's table, he kept the examination of them unto the elders of the church, as properly belonging unto their work and charge; and with his elders he would order them to make before the whole church a profession of a repenting faith, as they were able or willing to do it. Some, that could unto edification do it, he put upon thus relating the manner of their conversion to God; but usually they only answered unto certain probatory questions which were tendered them; and so after their names had been for a few weeks before signified unto the congregation, to learn whether any objection or exception could be made against them, of any thing scandalous in their conversations, now consenting unto the covenant, they were admitted into the church communion. As for ecclesiastical censures, he was very watchful to prevent all procedures unto them, as far as was consistent with the rules of our Lord; for which cause (except in grosser abominations) when offences happened, he did his utmost that the notice thereof might be extended no further than it was when they first were laid before him; and having reconciled the offenders with sensible and convenient acknowledgements of their miscarriages, he would let the notice thereof be confined unto such as were aforehand therewith acquainted; and hence there was but one person admonished in, and but one person excommunicated from, the church of Hartford, in all the fourteen years that Mr. Hooker lived there. He was much troubled at the too frequent censures in some other churches; and he would say, "Church censures are things wherewith neither we nor our fathers have been acquainted in the practice of them; and therefore the utmost circumspection is needful, that we do not spoil the ordinances of God by our management thereof."

He would say, "that he should esteem it a favour from God, if he might live no longer than he should be able to hold up lively in the work of his place; and that when the time of his departure should come, God would shorten the time;" and he had his desire. At last he closed his own eyes with his own hands, and gently stroking his own forehead, with a smile in his countenance, he gave a little groan, and so expired his blessed soul into the arms of his fellow-servants, the holy angels, on July 7, 1647.

Life of John Eliot

The natives of the country now possessed by the New-Englanders had been forlorn and wretched heathen ever since their first herding here; and though we know not when or how those Indians first became inhabitants of this mighty continent, yet we may guess that probably the devil decoyed those miserable salvages hither, in hopes that the gospel of the Lord Jesus Christ would never come here to destroy or disturb his absolute empire over them. But our Eliot was in such ill terms with the devil, as to alarm him with sounding the silver trumpets of Heaven in his territories, and make some noble and zealous attempts towards ousting him of ancient possessions here.

I cannot find that any besides the Holy Spirit of God first moved him to the blessed work of evangelizing these perishing Indians; it was that Holy Spirit which laid before his mind the idea of that which was on the seal of the Massachuset colony: a poor Indian having a label going from his mouth, with a COME OVER AND HELP US. It was the spirit of our Lord Jesus Christ, which enkindled in him a pitty for the dark souls of these natives, whom the "god of this world had blinded," through all the bypast ages. He was none of those that make "the salvation of the heathen" an article of their creed; but (setting aside the unrevealed and extraordinary steps which the "Holy One of Israel" may take out of his usual paths) he thought men to be lost if our gospel be hidden from them.

But when this charitable pitty had once began to flame, there was a concurrence of many things to cast oyl into it. All the good men in the country were glad of his engagement in such an undertaking; the ministers especially encouraged him, and those in the neighbourhood kindly supplyed his place, and performed his work in part for him at Roxbury, while he was abroad labouring among them that were without. Hereunto he was further awakened by those expressions in the royal charter, in the assurance and protection whereof this wilderness was first peopled; namely, "To win and incite the natives of that country to the knowledge and obedience of the only true God and Saviour of mankind, and the Christian faith, in our royal intention, and the adventurer's free profession is the principal end of the plantation." And the remarkable zeal of the Romish missionaries, "compassing sea and land, that they might make proselytes," made his devout soul think of it with a further disdain, that we should come any whit behind in our care to evangelize the Indians whom we dwelt among. Lastly, when he had well begun this evangelical business, the good God, in an answer to his prayers, mercifully stirred up a liberal contribution among the godly people in England for the promoting of it; by means whereof a considerable estate and income was at length entrusted in the hands of an honourable corporation, by whom it is to this day very carefully employed in the Christian service which it was designed for. And then, in short, inasmuch as our Lord Jesus had bestowed on us, our Eliot was gratefully and generously desirous to obtain for him "the heathen for an inheritance, and the utmost parts of the earth, for a possession."

It remains that I lay before the world the remarkable conduct and success of this famous man, in his great affair; and I shall endeavour to do it by Englishing and reprinting a letter, sent a while since by my father unto his learned and renowned correspondent, the venerable Dr. Leusden at Utrecht: which letter has already been published, if I mistake not, in four or five divers languages.

Worthy and Much Honoured Sir: Your letters were very grateful to me, by which I understand that you and others in your famous University of Utrecht desire to be informed concerning the converted Indians in America: take therefore a true account of them in a few words.

It is above forty years since that truly godly man, Mr. John Eliot, pastor of the church at Rocksborough, (about a mile from Boston in New-England,) being warmed with a holy zeal of converting the Americans, set himself to learn the Indian tongue, that he might more easily and successfully open to them the mysteries of the gospel, upon account of which he has been (and not undeservedly) called, "the Apostle of the American Indians." This reverend person, not without very great labour, translated the whole Bible into the Indian tongue; he translated also several English treatises of practical divinity and catechisms into their language. Above twenty six years ago he gathered a church of converted Indians in a town called Natick; these Indians confessed their sins with tears, and professed their faith in Christ, and afterwards they and their children were baptized, and they were solemnly joined together in a church-covenant; the said Mr. Eliot was the first that administered the Lord's Supper to them. The pastor of that church now is an Indian: his name is Daniel. Besides this church at Natick, among our inhabitants in the Massachusets Colony there are four Indian assemblies, where the name of the true God and Jesus Christ is solemnly called upon; these assemblies have some American preachers. Mr. Eliot formerly used to preach to them once every fortnight, but now he is weakned with labours and old age, being in the eighty-fourth year of his age, and preacheth not to the Indians oftener than once in two months.

There is another church, consisting only of converted Indians, about fifty miles from hence, in an Indian town called Mashippaug: the first pastor of that church was an

English man, who, being skilful in the American language, preached the gospel to them in their own tongue. This English pastor is dead, and instead of him, that church has an Indian-preacher.

There are, besides that, five assemblies of Indians proffessing the name of Christ, not far distant from Maship-paug, which have Indian preachers: John Cotton, pastor of the church at Plymouth, (son of my venerable father-in-law John Cotton, formerly the famous teacher of the church at Boston,) who made very great progress in learning the Indian tongue, and is very skilful in it; he preaches in their own language to the last five mentioned congregations every week. Moreover of the inhabitants of Saconet in Plymouth Colony, there is a great congregation of those who for distinction sake are called "praying Indians," because they pray to God in Christ.

Not far from a promontory called Cape Cod, there are six assemblies of heathens who are to be reckoned as catechu-mens, amongst whom there are six Indian preachers: Samuel Treat, pastor of a church at Eastham, preacheth to those congregations in their own language. There are likewise amongst the islanders of Nantucket a church, with a pastor who was lately a heathen, and several meetings of catechumens, who are instructed by the converted Indians. There is also another island, about seven leagues long, (called Martha's Vineyard,) where are two American church-es planted, which are more famous than the rest, over one of which there presides an ancient Indian as pastor, called Hiacooms: John Hiacooms, son of the Indian pastor, also preacheth the gospel to his countrymen. In another church in that place, John Tockinosh, a converted Indian, teaches. In these churches ruling elders of the Indians are joined to the pastors: the pastors were chosen by the people, and when they had fasted and prayed, Mr. Eliot and Mr. Cotton laid their hands on them, so that they were solemnly ordained. All the congregations of the converted Indians (both the catechumens and those in church order) every Lord's day meet together; the pastor or preacher always begins with prayer, and without a form, because from the heart; when the ruler of the assembly has ended prayer, the whole congregation of Indians praise God with singing; some of them are excellent singers: after the psalm, he that preaches reads a place of Scripture, (one or more verses as he will,) and expounds it, gathers doctrines from it, proves them by scriptures and reasons, and infers uses from them after the manner of the English, of whom they have been taught; then another prayer to God in the name of Christ concludes the whole service. Thus do they meet together twice every Lord's day. They observe no holy-days but the Lord's day, except upon some extraordinary occasion; and then they solemnly set apart whole days, either giving thanks or fasting and praying with great fervour of mind.

Before the English came into these coasts these barbarous nations were altogether ignorant of the true God; hence it is that in their prayers and sermons they use English words and terms; he that calls upon the most holy name of God, says, Jehovah, or God, or Lord, and also they have learned and borrowed many other theological phrases from us.

In short, "There are six churches of baptized Indians in New-England, and eighteen assemblies of catechumens, professing the name of Christ: of the Indians there are four-and-twenty who are preachers of the word of God, and besides these there are four English ministers, who preach the gospel in the Indian tongue." I am now my self weary with writing, and I fear lest, if I should add more, I should also be tedious to you; yet one thing I must add, which I had almost forgot, that there are many of the Indians' children who have learned by heart the catechism, either of that famous divine William Perkins, or that put forth by the assembly of divines at Westminster, and in their own mother tongue can answer to all the questions in it.

Book IV

THE SALT OF THE NATIONS:
A HISTORY OF HARVARD COLLEGE

The nations of mankind, that have shaken off barbarity, have not more differed in the languages, than they have agreed in this one principle, that schools, for the institution of young men, in all other liberal sciences, as well as that of languages, are necessary to procure, and preserve, that learning amongst them, which

Emollit mores, nec sinit esse feros[35]

America is the part of the world whereto our history is confined; and one little part of America, where the first academy that ever adorned any English plantation in America was erected; and an academy which, if *majores nostri academias signato vocabulo appellavere Universitates, quod Universarum Divinarum Humanarumque Rerum Cognitio, in ijs, ut Thesauro conservato aperiatur,*[36] it may, though it have otherwise wanted many priviledges, from the very foundation of it pretend unto the name of an university. The primitive Christians were not more prudently careful to settle schools for the education of persons, to succeed the more immediately inspired ministry of the apostles, and such as had been ordained by the apostles; (and the apostle Julian truly imagined that he could not sooner undo Christianity than by putting of them down!) than the Christians in the most early times of New-England were to form a colledge, wherein a succession of a learned and able ministry might be educated. And, indeed, they foresaw that without such a provision for a sufficient ministry, the churches of New-England must have been less than a business of one age, and soon have come to nothing: the other hemisphere of the world would never have sent us over men enough to have answered our necessities; but without a nursery for such men among ourselves "darkness must have soon covered the land, and gross darkness the people." For some little while, indeed, there were very hopeful effects of the pains taken by certain particular men of great worth and skill, to bring up some in their own private families for public services; but much of uncertainty and of inconveniency in this way was in that little while discovered; and when wise men considered the question handled by Quintilian, *Utilius ne sit domi, atque, intra privatos Parietes studentem continere, an frequentiae scholarum, et velut publicis praeceptoribus tradere?*[37] they soon determined it as he did, that set-schools are so necessary, there is no doing without them. Wherefore a colledge must now be thought upon: a colledge, the best thing that ever New-England thought upon! As the admirable Voctius could happily boast of it, that whereas there are no less than ten provinces in the Popish Belgium, and there are no more than two universities in them, there are but seven provinces in the reformed Belgium, and there are five universities therein, besides other academical societies; thus the first possessors of this Protestant and Puritan country were zealous for an university, that should be more significant than the seminaries of Canada and Mexico; New-England, compared with other places, might lay claim to the character that Strabo gives to Tarsus, the city of our apostle Paul's first education; "they had so great a love to Philosophy," (τοσαύτη σπʹςδὴ πρὸσ τε φιλοσοφίαν,) and all the liberal sciences, that they excelled Athens, Alexandria, and if there were any other place worth naming where the schools, and disputes of philosophy, and all humane arts are maintained."

A General Court, held at Boston, September 8, 1630, advanced a small sum (and it was then a day of small things), namely, four hundred pounds, by way of essay towards the building of something to begin a colledge; and New-Town being the *Kiriath Sepher*[38] appointed for the seat of it, the name of the town was for the sake of somewhat now founding here, which might hereafter grow into an university, changed into Cambridge. 'Tis true, the University of Upsal in Sueden hath ordinarily about seven or eight hundred students belonging to it, which do none of them live collegiately, but board all of them here and there at private houses; nevertheless, the government of New-England was for having their students brought up in a more collegiate way of living. But that which laid the most significant stone in the foundation, was the last will of Mr. John Harvard, a reverend and excellent minister of the gospel, who, dying at Charlestown of a consumption, quickly after his arrival here, bequeathed the sum of seven hundred, seventy nine pounds, seventeen shillings and two pence, towards the pious work of building a colledge, which was now set a foot.

A committee then being chosen, to prosecute an affair so happily commenced, it soon found encouragement from several other benefactors: the other colonies sent some small help to the undertaking, and several particular gentlemen did more than whole colonies to support and forward it: but because the memorable Mr. John Harvard led the way by a generosity exceeding the most of them that followed, his name was justly aeternized, by its having the name of Harvard Colledge imposed upon it. While these things were a doing, a society of scholars, to lodge in the new nests, were forming under the conduct of one Mr. Nathaniel Eaton, a blade who marvellously deceived the expectations of good men concerning him; for he was one fitter to be master of a bridewel than a colledge: and though his avarice was notorious enough to get the name of a *Philargyriius*[39] fixed upon him, yet his cruelty was more scandalous than his avarice. He was a rare scholar himself, and he made many more such; but their education truly was "in the school of Tyrannus." Among many other instances of his cruelty, he gave one in causing two men to hold a young gentleman, while he so unmercifully beat him with a cudgel, that, upon complaint of it unto the court in September, 1639, he was fined an hundred marks, besides a convenient sum to be paid unto the young gentleman that had suffered by his unmercifulness; and for his inhumane severities towards the scholars, he was removed from his trust.

On August 27, 1640, the magistrates, with the ministers, of the colony, chose Mr. Henry Dunstar to be the president of their new Harvard-Colledge. And in time convenient, the General Court endued the colledge with a charter, which made it a corporation, consisting of a president, two fellows, and a treasurer to all proper intents and purposes: only with powers reserved unto the governour, deputy-governour, and all the magistrates of the colony, and the ministers of the six next towns for the time being, to act as overseers or visitors of the society. The tongues and arts were now taught in the colledge, and piety was maintained with so laudable a discipline, that many eminent persons went forth from hence, adorned with accomplishments, that rendered them formidable to other parts of the world, as well as to this country, and persons of good quality sent their sons from other parts of the world for such an education as this country could give unto them. The number of benefactors to the colledge did herewithall increase to such a degree of benefits, that although the president were supported still by a salary from the treasury of the colony, yet the treasury of the colledge itself was able to pay many of its expences; especially after the incomes of Charlestown ferry were by an act of the General Court settled thereupon. And while these made their liberal contributions, either to the edifice or to the revenue of the colledge, there were other that enriched its library by presenting of choice books with mathematical instruments thereunto. Indeed this library is at this day, far from a Vatican, or a Bodleian dimension, and sufficiently short of that made by Ptolomy at Alexandria, in which fame hath placed seven hundred thousand volumes, and of that made by Theodosius at Constantinople, in which a more certain fame hath told us of ten myriads: nevertheless 'tis I suppose the best furnished that can be shown any where in all the American regions.

When scholars had so far profitted at the grammar schools that they could read any classical author into English, and readily make and speak true Latin, and write it in verse as well as prose; and perfectly decline the paradigms of nouns and verbs in the Greek tongue, they were judged capable of admission in Harvard-Colledge; and, upon the examination, were accordingly admitted by the president and fellows; who, in testimony thereof, signed a copy of the colledge laws, which the scholars were each of them to transcribe and preserve, as the continual remembrancers of the duties whereto their priviledges oblidged them. While the president inspected the manners of the students thus entertained in the colledge, and unto his morning and evening prayers in the hall joined an exposition upon the chapters; which they read out of Hebrew into Greek, from the Old Testament in the morning, and out of English into Greek, from the New Testament in the evening; besides what sermons he saw cause to preach in publick assemblies on the Lord's day at Cambridge where the students have a particular gallery allotted unto them; the fellows resident on the place became tutors to the several classes, and after they had instructed them in the Hebrew language, led them through all the liberal arts, ere their first four years expired. And in this time, they had their weekly declamations, on Fridays in the colledge-hall, besides publick disputations, which either the president or the fellows moderated. Those who then stood candidates to be graduates, were to attend in the hall for certain hours, on Mondays, and on Tuesdays, three weeks together towards the middle of June, which were called "weeks of visitation;" so that all comers that pleased might examine their skill in the languages and sciences which they now pretended unto; and usually, some or other of the over-seers of the colledge would on purpose visit them, whilst they were thus doing what they called "sitting of solstices:" when the commencement arrived — which was formerly the second Tuesday in August, but since, the first Wednesday in July — they that were to proceed bachelors, held their act publickly in Cambridge; whither the magistrates and minis-ters, and other gentlemen then came, to put respect upon their exercises: and these exercises were, besides an oration usually made by the president, orations both salutatory and valedictory, made by some or other of the commencers, wherein all persons and orders of any fashion then present, were addressed with proper complements, and reflections were made on the most remarkable occurrents of the praeceding year; and these orations were made not only in Latin, but sometimes in Greek and in Hebrew also; and some of them were in verse, and even in Greek verse, as well as others in prose. But the main exercises were dispu-tations upon questions, wherein the respondents first made their theses. In the close of the day, the president, with the formality of delivering a book into their hands, gave them their first degree: but such of them as had studied three years after their first degree, to answer the Horation charac-ter of an artist,

Qui Studiis Annos Septem dedit insenuitque
Libris et curis.[40]

And besides their exhibiting synopses of the liberal arts, by themselves composed, now again publickly disputed on some questions, of perhaps a little higher elevation; these now, with a like formality, received their second degree, proceeding masters of art.

Mr. Henry Dunster, continued the President of Harvard-Colledge, until his unhappy entanglement in the snares of Anabaptism fill'd the overseers with uneasie fears, lest the students, by his means, should come to be ensnared: Which uneasiness was at length so signified unto him, that on

October 24, 1654, he presented unto the overseers an instrument under his hands; wherein he resigned the presidentship, and they accepted his resignation. On November 2, 1654, Mr. Richard Mather and Mr. Norton were employed by the overseers to tender unto Mr. Charles Chancey the place of president, which was now become vacant; who, on the twenty-seventh day of that month, had a solemn inauguration thereunto.

After the death of Mr. Chancey, which was at the latter end of the year 1701, the *Alma Mater Academia* must look among her own sons, to find a president for the rest of her children; and accordingly the fellows of the colledge, with the approbation of the overseers, July 13, 1672, elected Mr. Leonard Hoar unto that office; whereto, on the tenth of September following, he was inaugurated. Were he considered either as a scholar or as a Christian, he was truly a worthy man; and he was generally reputed such, until happening, I can scarce tell how, to fall under the displeasure of some that made a figure in the neighbourhood, the young men in the colledge took advantage therefrom, to ruine his reputation, as far as they were able. The young plants turned cud-weeds, and, with great violations of the fifth Commandment, set themselves to travestie whatever he did and said, and aggravate every thing in his behaviour disagreeable to them, with a design to make him odious; and in a day of temptation, which was now upon them, several very good men did unhappily countenance the ungoverned youths in their ungovernableness. Things were at length driven to such a pass, that the students deserted the colledge, and the doctor, on March 15, 1675, resigned his presidentship.

After the death of Dr. Hoar, the place of president *pro tempore*, was put upon Mr. Urian Oakes, the excellent pastor of the church at Cambridge; who did so, and would no otherwise accept of the place; though the offer of a full settlement in the place was afterwards importunately made unto him. He did the services of a president, even, as he did all other services, faithfully, learnedly, indefatigably; and by a new choice of him thereunto, on February 2, 1679, was, at last, prevailed withal to take the full charge upon him.

Mr. Oakes being transplanted into the better world, the presidentship was immediately tendered unto Mr. Increase Mather; but his church, upon the application of the overseers unto them to dismiss him unto the place whereto he was now chosen, refusing to do it, he declined the motion. Wherefore, on April 10, 1682, Mr. John Rogers was elected unto that place; and on August 12, 1683, he was installed into it. But him also a praemature death, on July 2, 1684, the day after the commencement, snatcht away from a society that hoped for a much longer enjoyment of him, and counted themselves under as black an eclipse as the sun did happen to be, at the hour of his expiration.

The colledge was now again, by universal choice, cast into the hands of Mr. Increase Mather, who had already, in other capacities, been serving of it; and he accordingly, without leaving either his house or his church at Boston, made his continual visits to the colledge at Cambridge, managing as well the weekly disputation, as the annual commencements, and inspecting the whole affairs of the society; and by preaching often at Cambridge, he made his visits yet more profitable unto them.

Reader, the interest and figure which the world knows this my parent hath had, in the ecclesiastical concerns of this country, ever since his first return from England in the twenty-second, until his next return from England in the fifty-third year of his age; makes it a difficult thing for me to write the church-history of the country. Should I insert every where the relation which he hath had unto the public matters, it will be thought by the envious that I had undertaken this work with an eye to such a motto as the son of the memorable prince of Orange took his device, *patri-aeque patrique*:[41] should I, on the other side, bury in utter silence all the effects of that care and zeal wherewith he

hath employed in his peculiar opportunities, with which
the gree grace of Heaven hath talented him to do good
unto the public; I must cut off some essentials of my story.
Wherefore I will not only add in this place, that when the
honourable Joseph Dudley, Esq., was by the king's commission made President of the territory of New-England, this
gentleman, among other expressions of his hearty desire to
secure the prosperity of his mother, whose breasts himself
had sucked, continued the government of the colledge in
the hands of Mr. Mather, and altered his title into that of a
rector. But when wise persons apprehended that the constitution of men and things, which followed after the arrival
of another governor, threatened all the churches with quick
ruines, wherein the colledge could not but be comprehend-
ed, Mr. Mather did, by their advice, repair to Whitehall;
where, being remarkably favoured by three crowned heads,
in successive and personal applications unto them, on the
behalf of his distressed country, and having obtained several kindnesses for the colledge in particular, he returned
into New-England, in the beginning of the year, 1692, with
a royal charter, full of most ample privileges. By that royal
charter, under the seal of King William and Queen Mary,
the country had its English and its Christian liberties, as
well as its titles to its lands (formerly contested) secured to
it; and the province being particularly enabled hereby to
incorporate the colledge, (which was the reason that he did
not stay to solicit a particular charter for it,) immediately
upon his arrival the general assembly gratified his desire, in
granting a charter to this university. Mr. Mather now
reassuming the quality of president over the colledge,
which in his absence had flourished for divers years, under
the prudent government of two tutors, Mr. John Leveret
and Mr. William Bruttle, he does to this day continue his
endeavours to keep alive that river, the streams whereof
have made glad this city of God.

Book V

ACTS AND MONUMENTS:
THE NEW ENGLAND WAY

The Faith of the Churches

It was once an unrighteous and injurious aspersion cast upon the churches of New-England, that "the world knew not their principles:" whereas they took all the occasions imaginable to make all the world know, "that in the doctrinal part of religion, they have agreed entirely with the reformed churches of Europe:" and that they desired most particularly to maintain the faith professed by the churches of Old England, the country whereto was owing their original. Few pastors of mankind ever took such pains at catechising, as have been taken by our New-English divines. Now, let any man living read the most judicious and elaborate catechisms published, and say whether true divinity were ever better handled; or whether they were not the truest sons of the church of England, who thus maintained its "fundamental articles," which are so many of them first subscribed, and then denied and confuted by some that would monopolize that name unto themselves: but as a further demonstration thereof, when there was a synod assembled at Cambridge, September 30, 1648, even that synod which framed, agreed and published, "the Platform of Church-discipline," there was a most unanimous vote passed in these words:

> "This synod having perused and considered (with much gladness of heart and thankfulness to God) the 'confession of faith,' published by the late reverend assembly in England, do judge it to be very holy, orthodox and

judicious, in all matters of faith, and do therefore freely and fully consent thereunto for the substance thereof. Only in those things which have respect to church-government and discipline, we refer ourselves to the 'Platform of Church-discipline,' agreed upon by this present assembly: and we do therefore think it meet that this confession of faith should be commended to the churches of Christ among us, and to the honoured court, as worthy of their due consideration and acceptance."

This vote was passed by the ministers and messengers of the churches, in that venerable assembly, when the government recommended unto their consideration, "a confession of faith," as one thing, which the transmarine churches expected from them. And they hoped that this proof of them being "fellow heirs of the same common salvation" with the churches beyond sea, would not only free them from the suspicion of heresie, but clear them from the character of schism also; in as much as their dissent from those churches, was now evidently but in some lesser matters of ecclesiastical polity; and a dissent not managed either with such arrogancy or censoriousness as are the essential properties of schismaticks.

As to make "a confession of faith," is a duty wherein all Christians are to be made confessors, and multitudes of 'em have been made martyrs; thus to write "a confession of faith," is a work which the faithful in all ages have approved and practised, as most singularly profitable. How remarkably the confessions of the four general councils were owned for the suppression of the heresies then spawned, is well known to all that have set foot but as far as the threshold of church-history; and surely the fabulous musick of the spheres cannot be supposed more delicious than that harmony which is to be seen in the confessions of the reformed churches, that have therefore been together published. Wherefore, besides the vote of the New-England churches, for a concurrence with the confession of faith made by the assembly at Westminster, a synod assembled at Boston, May 12, 1680, whereof Mr. Increase Mather was moderator, consulted and considered what was further to be done for such a confession. Accordingly, the confession of faith consented by the congregational churches of England in a synod met at the Savoy, which, excepting a few variations, was the same with what was agreed by the reverend assembly at Westminster, and afterwards by the general assembly of Scotland; was twice publickly read, examined and approved; and some small variations made from that of the Savoy, in compliance with that at Westminster; and so, after such collations, but no contentions, voted and printed, as the faith of New-England.

The Discipline of the Churches

The churches of New-England enjoying so much rest and growth as they had now seen, for some sevens of years, it was, upon many accounts, necessary for them to make such a declaration of the church-order, wherein the good hand of God had moulded 'em, as might convey and secure the like order unto the following generations. Next unto the Bible, which was the professed, perpetual and only directory of these churches, they had no platform of their church-government, more exact than their famous John Cotton's well-known book of "The Keys;" which book endeavours to lay out the just lines and bounds of all church power, and so defines the matter, that, as in the state, there is a dispersion of powers into several hands which are to concur in all acts of common concernment; from whence ariseth the healthy constitution of a common-wealth; in like sort, he assigns the power in the church unto several subjects, wherein the united light of Scripture and of Nature have placed them, with a very satisfactory distribution. He asserts that a presbyterated society of the faithful hath within itself a compleat power of self-reformation, or, if you will, of self-preservation, and may within itself manage its own choices of officers and censures of delinquents. Now, a special statute-law of our Lord having excepted women and children from enjoying any part of this power, he finds only

elders and brethren to be the constituent members, who
may act in such a sacred corporation; the elders, he finds
the first subject entrusted with government, the brethren
endowed with priviledge, insomuch, that tho' the elders
only are to rule the church, and without them there can be
no elections, admissions, or excommunications, and they
have a negative upon the acts of the fraternity, as well as
'tis they only that have the power of authoritative
preaching, and administring the sacraments; yet the brethren have such a liberty, that without their consent nothing of common concernment may be imposed upon them.
Nevertheless, because particular churches of elders and
brethren may abuse their power with manifold miscarriages, he asserts the necessary communion of churches in
synods, who have authority to determine, declare and in-
join, such things as may rectifie the male-administrations,
or any disorders, dissentions and confusions of the congregations, which fall under their cognizance: but, still, so as
to leave unto the particular churches themselves the formal
acts, which are to be done pursuant unto the advice of the
council; upon the scandalous and obstinate refusal whereof, the council may determine "to withdraw communion
from them," as from those who will not be counselled
against a notorious mismanagement of the jurisdiction
which the Lord Jesus Christ has given them. This was the
design of that judicious treatise, wherein was contained the
substance of our church-discipline. But it was convenient
the churches of New-England should have a system of their
discipline, extracted from the word of God, and exhibited
unto them, with a more effectual, acknowledged and established recommendation: and nothing but a council was
proper to compose the system.

Wherefore, a bill was preferred unto the General Court in
the year 1646, for the calling of a synod, whereby, a "platform of church discipline," according to the direction of
our Lord Jesus Christ in his blessed word, might most
advantageously be composed and published. The magis-

trates in the General Court passed the bill, but the deputies had their little scruples how far the civil authority might interpose in matters of such religious and ecclesiastical cognizance; and whether scaffolds might not now be raised, by the means whereof the civil authority should pretend hereafter to impose an uniformity, in such instances which had better be left at liberty and variety. It was reply'd, that it belong'd unto magistrates by all rational ways to encourage truth and peace among their people; and that the council now called by the magistrates was to proceed but by way of council, with the best light which could be fetched from the word of God; but the court would be after all free, as they saw cause to approve or to reject what should be offered.

After all, tho' the objections of the deputies were thus answered, yet, in compliance with such as were not yet satisfied, the order for the calling of the intended assembly was directed only in the form of a motion, and not of a command, unto the churches. But certain persons, come lately from England, so inflamed the zeal for "liberty of conscience" among the people, that all this compliance of the authority could not remove the fear of some churches, lest some invasion of that liberty were threatened by a clause in the order of the court, which intimated "that what should be presented by the synod, the court would give such allowance as would be meet unto it." The famous and leading church of Boston, particularly, was ensnared so much by this fear, that upon the Lord's day, when the "order of the court" was first communicated unto them, they could not come unto an immediate resolution of sending any delegates unto the synod; but Mr. Norton, then of Ipswich, at Boston lecture the Thursday following, preached an elaborate sermon unto a vast auditory, on Moses and Aaron kissing each other in the mount of God: and in that sermon, he so represented the nature and power of synods, and the respect owing from churches to rulers calling for synods, that on the next Lord's day, the church voted the sending of three messengers, with their elders, unto this assembly.

It being so near winter before the synod could convene, that few of the ministers invited from the other colonies could be present at it, they now sat but fourteen days; and then adjourned unto the eighth of June in the year ensuing. Nevertheless, at their first session, there was an occasion which they took to consider and examine an important case; and it came to this result:

> "The civil magistrate in matters of religion, or of the first table, hath power civilly to command or forbid things respecting the outward man which are clearly commanded or forbidden in the word, and to inflict suitable punishments, according to the nature of the transgressions against the same."

But the "platform of church discipline" to be commended unto the churches, was the main chance which the assembly was to mind; in order whereunto they directed three eminent persons — namely, Mr. John Cotton, Mr. Richard Mather, and Mr. Ralph Partridge — each of them to draw up a scriptural "model of church government;" unto the end that, out of those, there might be one educed, which the synod might, after the most filing thoughts upon it, send abroad. When the synod met, at the time to which they had adjourned, the summer proved so sickly that a delay of one year more was given to their undertaking; but at last the desired "platform of church discipline" was agreed upon, so it was presented unto the General Court, in the month of October, 1648. And the court most thankfully accepted and approved of it.

The Half-Way Covenant

As the English nation has been honoured above most of the Protestant and reformed world, with clearer discoveries of several most considerable points in our Christian religion — particularly the points of a true evangelical church-order — so the New-English part of this nation hath had a singular share in receiving and imparting the illuminations which the light shining in a dark place hath given thereabout.

It might rationally be now expected that our compassionate Lord Jesus Christ would graciously gratifie the desires and labours of such an holy generation with as full an understanding of his revealed will about his instituted worship as he has at any time granted unto any of his people, and that especially the officers of instituted churches — humbly prayerfully and carefully engaged in studies for their service — would lye under as direct an influence of his Holy Spirit, as any inquirers whatsoever. But there is one very important article of ecclesiastical discipline whereabouts the churches of New-England have had a most peculiar exercise and concernment; and that is "the ecclesiastical state of their posterity."

When our churches were come to between twenty and thirty years of age, a numerous posterity was advanced so far into the world, that the first planters began apace in their several families to be distinguished by the name of grand-fathers; but among the immediate parents of the grandchildren, there were multitudes of well disposed persons, who, partly thro' their own doubts and fears, and partly thro' other culpable neglects, had not actually come up to the covenanting state of communicants at the table of the Lord. The good old generation could not, without many uncomfortable apprehensions, behold their off-spring excluded from the baptism of Christianity, and from the ecclesiastical inspection which is to accompany that baptism; indeed, it was to leave their off-spring under the shepherdly government of our Lord Jesus Christ in his ordinances, that they had brought their lambs into his wilderness. When the apostle bids churches to "look diligently, lest any man fail of the grace of God," there is an ecclesiastical word used for that "looking diligently;" intimating that God will ordinarily bless a regular church-watch, to maintain the interests of grace among his people:

and it was therefore the study of those prudent men, who might be call'd our seers, that the children of the faithful may be kept, as far as may be, under a church-watch, in expectation that they might be in the fairer way to receive the grace of God; thus they were "looking diligently," that the prosperous and prevailing condition of religion in our churches might not be *Res unius aetatis,* — "a matter of one age alone." Moreover, among the next sons or daughters descending from that generation, there was a numerous appearance of sober persons, who professed themselves desirous to renew their baptismal-covenant and submit unto the church-discipline, and so have their houses also marked for the Lord's; but yet they could not come up to that experimental account of their own regeneration, which would sufficiently embolden their access to the other sacrament. Wherefore, for our churches now to make no ecclesiastical difference between these hopeful candidates and competents for those our further mysteries, and Pagans, who might happen to hear the word of God in our assemblies, was judged a most unwarrantable strictness, which would quickly abandon the biggest part of our country unto heathenism. And, on the other side, it was feared that, if all such as had not yet exposed themselves by censurable scandals found upon them, should be admitted unto all the priviledges in our churches, a wordly part of mankind might, before we are aware, carry all things into such a course of proceeding, as would be very disagreeable unto the kingdom of heaven.

The questions raised about these matters came to some figures, first, in the colony of Connecticut; where the pious magistrates, observing the begun dangers of paroxysms, which might affect the state as well as the church, on this occasion produced a draught of the agitated questions, and sent them to the magistrates of the Massachusett's colony, with a request that several of the ablest ministers in both colonies might, upon mature deliberation, give in their answers thereunto. Accordingly, the letters of the government procured an assembly of our principal ministers at Boston, on June 4, 1657, who by the 19th of that month prepared and presented an elaborate answer to twenty-one questions; which was afterwards printed in London, under the title of "A Disputation concerning Church-members and their Children." Besides other cases referring to the church-state of children born in the bosom of the church, it is in this disputation asserted and maintained —

> "That it is the duty of infants, who confederate in their parents, when grown up unto years of discretion, tho' not yet fit for the Lord's Supper, to own the covenant they made with their parents, by entering thereinto in their own persons; and it is the duty of the church to call upon them for the performance thereof; and if, being called upon, they shall refuse the performance of this great duty, or otherwise do continue scandalous, they are liable to be censured for the same by the church. And in case they understand the "grounds of religion," and are not scandalous, and solemnly own the covenant, in their own persons, wherein they give up both themselves and their children unto the Lord, and desire baptism for them, we see not sufficient cause to deny baptism unto their children."

The practice of church care about the children of our churches thus directed and commended, was but gradually introduced; yea, it met with such opposition as could not be encountred with any thing less than a synod of elders and messengers from all the churches in the Massachuset colony. Accordingly, the General Court, having the necessity of the matter laid before them, at their second session in the year 1661, issued out their desire and order for the convening of such a synod at Boston in the spring of the year ensuing. And for the deliberations of that synod, besides the grand question about "the subject of baptism," there was another question propounded about "the consociation of churches," which was of no small consequence to the interests of Christianity in the country. As the divines of New-England were solicitous that the propagation of our churches might hold pace with that of our offspring, so they were industrious for the combination of our churches into such a bundle of arrowes as might not easily be broken. However, they had by their adversaries been termed independents; nevertheless, they solemnly on this occasion repeated and subscribed that profession of their famous brethren in the English nation:

"That it is the most to be abhorred maxim, that any religion hath made profession of, and therefore of all other the most contradictory, and dishonourable unto that of Christianity that a single and particular society of men, professing the name of Christ, and pretending to be endowed with a power from Christ, to judge them that are of the same body and society with themselves, should further arrogate unto themselves an exemption from giving account, or being censurable by any other, either Christian magistrate above them, or neighbour churches about them."

Under the influence of these concernments, the elders and messengers of the churches assembled at Boston, in the year 1662; who, under the conduct of several successive moderators, at length agreed upon certain propositions; which being tendered unto the General Court, there was an order there passed on October 8, 1662, for the publication and commendation thereof unto all the churches in the jurisdiction.

Reform Efforts

The settlement of the New-English churches, with a long series of preserving and prosperous smiles from Heaven upon them, is doubtless to be reckoned amongst the more "wonderful works of God," in this age; the true glories of the young plantation had not upon the face of God's earth a parallel, our adversaries themselves being judges. But when people began more notoriously to forget the "errand into the wilderness," and when the enchantments of this world caused the rising generation more sensibly to neglect the primitive designs and interests of religion propounded by their fathers; a change in the tenour of the divine dispensations towards this country, was quickly the matter of every body's observation. By land, some of the principle grains, especially our wheat and our pease, fell under an unaccountable blast, from which we are not, even unto this day, delivered; and besides that constant frown of Heaven upon our husbandry, recurring every year, few years have passed, wherein either worms or droughts, or some consuming disasters have not befallen the "labour of the husbandman." By sea, we were visited with multiplied shipwrecks, enemies prey'd on our vessels and sailors, and the affairs of the merchant were clogged with losses abroad; or fires, breaking forth in the chief seats of trade at home, wasted their substance with yet more costly desolations. Nor did the land and the sea more proclaim the controversie of our God against us, than that other element of the air, by the contagious vapours whereof several pestilential sicknesses did sometimes become epidemical among us. Yea, the judgments of God having done first the part of the moth upon us, proceeded then to do the part of a lion, in lamentable wars, wherein the barbarous Indians cruelly butchered many hundreds of our inhabitants, and scattered whole towns with miserable ruins.

The serious people throughout the country were awakened by these intimations of divine displeasure, to enquire into the causes and matters of the controversie. And besides the self-reforming effects of these calamities on the hearts and lives of many particular Christians, who were hereby brought unto an exacter walk with God, particular churches exerted their power of self-reformation, especially in the time of the Indian war; wherein with much solemn fasting and prayer, they renewed their covenants with God and one another. Moreover, the General Courts enacted what laws were judged proper for the extinction of those provoking evils, which might expose the land unto the anger of Heaven: and the ministers in their several congregations, by their ministry, set themselves to testifie against those evils. Nor is it a thing unworthy of a great remark, that great successes against the enemy accompanied some notable transactions both in church and in court, for the reformation of our provoking evils. Indeed, the people of God in this land were not gone so far in degeneracy, but that there were further degrees of disorder and corruption to be found — I must freely speak it — in other, yea, in all other places, where the Protestant religion is professed: and the most impartial observers must have acknowledged, that there was proportionably still more of true religion, and a larger number of the strictest saints in this country, than in any other on the face of the earth. But it was to be confessed, that the degeneracy of New-England, in any measure, into the spirit of the world, was a thing extreamly aggravated, by the greatness of our obligations to the contrary, and even sinful omissions in this, were no less criminal than the most odious commissions in some other countries.

After peace was restored unto the country, the evil spirit of apostacy from the "power of Godliness," and the various discoveries and consequences of such an apostasie, became still more sensible to them that "feared God." Wherefore, that there might be made a more exact scrutiny into the causes of the divine displeasure against the land, and into the methods of removing and preventing the matter of lamentation, and that the essays of reformation might be as well more extensive as more effectual than they had been hitherto, the General Court of the Massachusetts colony were prevailed withal to call upon the churches, that they would send their elders and other messengers to meet in a synod, for the solemn discussion of those two questions: "What are the provoking evils of New-England?" and, "What is to be done, that so those evils may be reformed?"

The churches, having first kept a general fast, that the gracious presence and spirit of God might be outlined for the direction of the approaching synod, the synod convened at Boston, September 10, 1679, chusing Mr. John Shermon and Mr. Urian Oakes for joint moderators during the biggest part of the session. The assembly kept a day of prayer with fasting before the Lord, and spent several days in discoursing upon the two grand questions laid before them, with utmost liberty granted unto every person to express his thoughts thereupon. A committee was appointed then to draw up the mind of the assembly; which being done, it was read over once and again, and each paragraph distinctly weighed, and then, upon a mature deliberation, the whole was unanimously voted, as to the substance, end and scope thereof. So 'twas presented unto the General Court, who by an act of October 15, 1679, "commended it unto the serious consideration of all the churches and people in the jurisdiction, enjoining and requiring all persons in their respective capacities to a careful and diligent reformation of all those provoking evils mentioned therein, according to the true intent thereof, that so the anger and displeasure of God, many ways manifested, might be averted, and his favour and blessing obtained."

That a reforming synod could not accomplish an universal reformation of provoking evils in the country, has been acknowledged as a matter of most sensible observation; and the increased frowns of Heaven upon the country, since that synod, have been but agreeable to such an increase of provocation. Our manifold indispositions to recover the dying "power of godliness," was punished with successive calamities; under all of which our apostacies from that godliness have rather proceeded than abated. Although there hath been a glorious profession of religion made by the body of this people unto this day; yea, and although there be thousands which by "keeping their hearts with all diligence," and by "ordering their conversations aright," justifie their profession, yet the number of them that so strictly "walk with God," has been wofully decaying. The old spirit of New-England hath been sensibly going out of the world, as the old saints in whom it was have gone; and instead thereof the spirit of the world, with a lamentable neglect of strict piety, has crept in upon the rising generation.

Book VI

A BOOK OF MEMORABLE EVENTS

To regard the illustrious displays of that providence where-with our Lord Christ governs the world, is a work, than which there is none more needful or useful for a Christian: to record them is a work, than which, none more proper for a minister: and perhaps the Great Governour of the world will ordinarily do the most notable things for those who are most ready to take a wise notice of what he does. Unaccountable therefore and inexcusable is the sleepiness, even upon the most of good men throughout the world, which indisposes them to observe and much more to preserve the remarkable dispensations of divine providence towards themselves or others. Nevertheless, there have been raised up, now and then, those persons who have rendered themselves worthy of everlasting remembrance, by their wakeful zeal to have the memorable providences of God remembred through all generations.

The like holy design was, by the Reverend Increase Mather, proposed among the divines of New-England, in the year 1681, at a general meeting of them; who thereupon desired him to begin, and publish an essay; which he did in a little while; but therewithal declared, "that he did it only as a specimen of a larger volume, in hopes that this work, being so set on foot, posterity would go on with it."

But as the national synods in France could not, by their frequent admonitions unto the churches to procure a good register of remarkable providences, effectually rouze their good men out of their stupidity, so the pastors in the churches of New-England have mostly been too much under the power of a like indisposition, to "regard the works of the Lord and the operation of his hands." That this indisposition might, if it were possible, be shaken off, there were proposals again made and sent thro' the country.

Tho' we have been too slack in doing what hath been desired and directed in these proposals, yet our church history is become able to entertain the world with a collection of remarkable providences that have occurr'd among the inhabitants of New-England. Besides a considerable number of memorables, which lie scatter'd here and there in every part of our church-history, there is a number of them, enough to make an intire book by themselves; whereof having received sufficient attestations, I shall now invite the reader to consider them.

A Wonderful Sea Deliverance

They "that go down to the sea in ships, these do see the works of the Lord, and his wonders in the deep." And what if our collection of remarkable providences do begin with a relation of the wonderful works which have been done for them that "go down to the sea in ships," by that great Lord "whose is the sea, for he made it?" I will carry my reader upon the huge Atlantick, and, without so much as the danger of being made sea-sick, he shall see "wonders in the deep."

Among remarkable sea-deliverances, no less than three several writers have published that wherein Major Edward Gibbons of Boston in New-England was concerned. A vessel bound from Boston to some other parts of America was, through the continuance of contrary winds, kept so long at sea, that the people aboard were in extream straits for want of provisions; and seeing that nothing here below could afford them any relief, they look'd upwards unto Heaven in humble and fervent supplications. The winds continuing still as they were, one of the company made a sorrowful motion that they should by a lot single out one to die, and by death to satisfie the ravenous hunger of the rest. After many a doleful and fearful debate upon this motion, they come to a result, that it must be done! The lot is cast; one of the company is taken; but where is the executioner that shall do the terrible office upon a poor innocent? It is a death now to think who shall act this bloody part in the tragedy; but before they fall upon this involuntary and unnatural execution, they once more went unto their zealous prayers; and, behold! while they were calling upon God, he answer'd them: for there leaped a mighty fish into their boat, which, to their double joy, not only quieted their outrageous hunger, but also gave them some token of a further deliverance. However, the fish is quickly eaten; the horrible famine returns, the horrible distress is renew'd; a black despair again seizes their spirits; for another morsel they come to a second lot, which fell upon another person; but still they cannot find an executioner: they once again fall to their importunate prayers: and behold, a second answer from above! A great bird lights and fixes itself upon the mast: one of the men spies it; and there it stands until he took it by the wing with his hand. This was a second life from the dead. This fowl, with the omen of a further deliverance in it, was a sweet feast unto them. Still their disappointments follow them; they can see no land, they know not where they are; irresistible hunger once more pinches them; they have no hope to be saved, but by a third miracle: they return to another lot; but before they go to the heart-breaking task of slaying the person under designation, they repeat their addresses unto the God of heaven, their former "friend in adversity." And now they look, and look again, but there is nothing: their devotions are concluded, and nothing appears: yet they hoped, yet they stayed, yet they lingered. At last one of 'em spies a ship, which put a new hope and life into 'em all. They bear up with their ship, they man their long-boat, they beg to board their vessel, and are admitted. It proves a French pirate. Major Gibbons petitions for a little bread, and offers all for it; but the commander was one who had formerly received considerable kindnesses of Major Gibbons at Boston, and now replied chearfully, "Major Gibbons, not a hair of you or your company shall perish, if it lies in my power to preserve you." Accordingly he supplied their necessities, and they made a comfortable end of their voyage.

Remarkable Conversions

The substance of the church, that mystical body of our Lord Jesus Christ, was from all eternity under the eye of God, as proposed in the decree of election. The members of that body were from all eternity written in the book of life: And, in pursuance of the divine decree concerning it, the Holy Spirit in the continuance of time, thro' several generations does fashion it into the shape designed for it. But how? We are told in Psal. CXXXIX. 14, " 'Tis fearfully and wondrously made; marvellous are the works of God about it." The marvellous works of God in converting and uniting of elect sinners unto the Lord Jesus Christ, will make an history for heaven. But something of that history has thousands of times been given to particular flocks of the faithful throughout New-England, in the relations which devout people have made unto them, at their first admission into their communion.

These marvellous works of God were very proper materials for a church-history: But ours has not a room for them; nor will I recite in this place more than two or three remarkables.

It was a problem among the ancient philosophers, "Whether a child may not confer more benefits on his father than he has received from him?" This hath been sometimes bravely determined in the affirmative among us, when fathers have by the means of their own children been born again.

One of my neighbours had a son which died when he was about five or six years old. The man's religion extended no further than to prayer with his family on the Lord's Days.

All the rest of the week his worldly heart was by the cares of this world indisposed for devotions. The mother of the child therefore pray'd with her children every day; and she saw the good effects of it upon them. This child lay sick for divers weeks; in which time he often called on his mother to pray for him — never on his father. And when the Lord's-Day arrived, the child would, with observable joy, utter that expression, "This is the day on which my father uses to go to prayer." The words of the dying son so stuck in the mind of his father, that with many tears he not only bewailed and reformed this his neglect of his family-prayer, but also became, as far as could be judged, a sincerely Godly man, dying afterwards in the fear of God.

Reader, pass thy judgments on a thing that is newly hapned. The story is published among us, and no body doth, or can doubt the truth of it. In Barwick, of our New-England, there dwelt one Ephraim Joy, as infamous a drunkard as perhaps any in the world. By his drunkenness he not only wasted his estate, but ruined his body too. At last, being both poor and sick, and therewithal hurried by sore temptations, a gentleman of Portsmouth, out of pure charity and compassion, took him into his house. While he lay ill there, the approaches of death and hell, under his convictions of his debauch'd life, exceedingly terrified him. Amidst these terrours, he dreamt that he made his appearance before the tribunal of the Lord Jesus Christ, the judge of the world, by whom he was condemned; whereupon he had a sight of the horrors in the state of damnation, which was now arresting of him. He cried with an anguish of importunity unto the judge for a pardon; but his eternal Judge answered him, that he would not yet give him an absolute pardon, but allow him fourteen days to repent; in which time, if he did repent, he should have a pardon. He dreamt that accordingly he repented and was pardon'd, and at the fourteen days' end received into heaven. The poor man declared his dream to the people of the house, and sent for the help of ministers and other Christians; and expressed the humiliations of a very deep repentance. As he drew near his end, he grew daily more lively in the exercises of his faith on the Lord Jesus Christ, relying on him for salvation; until he confidently said that his peace was made with God. But, behold, at the expiration of the fourteen days, precisely and exactly according to his dream, he died. Yea, and he died full of that great joy which gave no little to the spectators.

A Criminal's Dying Speech

It hath been thought, that the dying speeches of such as have been executed among us, might be of singular use to correct and reform the crimes wherein too many do live: and it has been wish'd that at least some fragments of those dying speeches might be preserv'd and publish'd. Upon this advice from some good persons, I have stollen an hour or two, wherein I have collected some accounts of several ill persons, which have been cut off by the sword of civil justice in this land; and this collection I suffer to go abroad, in hopes that, among many other essays to suppress growing vice, it may signifie something with the blessing of Heaven thereupon, to let the vicious understand what have been the cries of our miserables when passing into another world. Behold, an history of criminals, whom the terrible judgments of God have thunder-strook into pillars of salt.

An English ship (in the year 1673) sailing from somewhere about the mouth of the Streights, was mann'd with some cruel miscreants, who, quarrelling with the master and some of the officers, turn'd them all into the long boat, with a small quantity of provisions, about an hundred leagues to the westward of the Spanish coast.

These fellows, in the mean time, set sail for New-England; where, by a surprising providence of God, the master, with his afflicted company in the long boat, also arrived; all, except one, who died of the barbarous usage.

The countenance of the master was now come terrible to the rebellious men, who, though they had escap'd the sea, yet "vengeance would not suffer to live a-shore." At his instance and complaint, they were apprehended; and the ringleaders of this murderous piracy had a sentence of death executed on them in Boston.

Under that sentence, there was heard among them a grievous lamentation for this: "Their education had been under the means of grace, and the faithful preaching of the gospel in England; but they had sinned against that education." And one of them sadly cry'd out, "Oh! 'tis my drunkenness, 'tis my drunkenness, that hath brought me to this lamentable end!"

The horrors which attended the chief of these malefactors (one Forrest) in the last hours of his life, were such as exceedingly astonished the beholders. Though he were a very stout man, yet now his trembling agonies and anguishes were inexpressible. One speech, let fall by him, was, "I have been among drawn swords, flying bullets, roaring cannons — amidst all which, I knew not what fear meant; but now I have dreadful apprehensions of the dreadful wrath of God in the other world, which I am going into, my soul within me is amazed at it."

Wonders of the Invisible World

Molestations from evil spirits, in more sensible and surprising operations, than those finer methods, wherein they commonly work upon the minds of all men, but especially of ill men, have so abounded in this countrey, that I question whether any one town has been free from sad examples of them. The neighbours have not been careful enough to record and attest the prodigious occurrences of this importance, which have been among us. Many true and strange occurrences from the invisible world, in these parts of the world, are faultily buried in oblivion. But some of these very stupendous things have had their memory preserv'd in the written memorials of honest, prudent, and faithful men; whose veracity in the relations cannot without great injury be question'd.

In the latter end of the year 1691, Mr. Paris, pastor of the church in Salem-Village, had a daughter of nine, and a niece of about eleven years of age, sadly afflicted of they knew not what distempers: and tho' he made his application to physicians, yet still they grew worse. At length one physician gave his opinion that "they were under an evil hand." This the neighbours took up, and concluded they were bewitch'd. He had also an Indian man-servant and his wife, who afterwards confess'd that, without the knowledge of their master or mistress, they had taken some of the afflicted person's urine, and mixing it with meal, had made a cake, and baked it, to find out the witch, as they said. After this, the afflicted persons cry'd out of the Indian woman named Tituba, that she did pinch, prick, and grievously torment them; and that they saw her here and there, where no body else could; yea, they could tell where she was, and what she did, when out of their humane sight. These children were bitten and pinch'd by invisible agents; their arms, necks, and backs turn'd this way and that way, and return'd back again; so as it was impossible for them to do of themselves, and beyond the power of any epileptick fits or natural diseases to effect. Sometimes they were taken dumb, their mouths stopp'd, their throats choak'd, their limbs rack'd and tormented, so as might move an heart of stone to sympathise with them, with bowels of compassion for them.

Mr. Paris, seeing the distress'd condition of his family, desired the presence of some worthy gentlemen of Salem, and some neighbour-ministers, to consult together at his house; who, when they came, and had inquir'd diligently into the sufferings of the afflicted, concluded they were preternatural, and fear'd the hand of Satan was in them. In a short time after, other persons who were of age to be witnesses, were molested by Satan, and in their fits cry'd out upon Tituba, and Goody O. and S.G. that they, or spectres in their shape, did grievously torment them. Some of their village-neighbours complain'd unto the magistrates at

Salem, desiring they would come and examine the afflicted
and the accused together; the which they did: the effect of
which examination was, that Tituba confess'd she was a
witch; and that she, with the two others accus'd, did torment and bewitch the complainers; and that these, with
two others, whose names she knew not, had their witch-
meetings together, relating the times when, and places
where, they met, with many other circumstances elsewhere
to be seen at large. Upon this, the said Tituba and O. and
G. were committed to prison upon suspicion of acting
witchcraft. After this, the said Tituba was again examin'd
in prison, and own'd her first confession in all points, and
then was herself afflicted, and complain'd of her fellow-
witches tormenting of her for her confession, and accusing
them; and being search'd by a woman, she was found to
have upon her body the marks of the devil's wounding her.

I observ'd, in the prosecution of these affairs, that there
was in the justices, judges, and others concern'd, a conscientious endeavour to do the thing that was right; and to that
end, they consulted the precedents of former times, and
precepts laid down by learn'd writers about witchcraft.

But that which chiefly carry'd on this matter to such an
height was the increasing of confessors until they amounted
to near upon fifty; and four or six of them upon their trials
own'd their guilt of this crime, and were condemn'd for the
same, but not executed. And many of the confessors
confirmed their confessions with very strong circumstances;
as their exact agreement with the accusations of the afflicted, their punctual agreement with their fellow-confessors,
their relating the times when they covenanted with Satan,
and the reasons that mov'd 'em thereunto; their witch-
meetings, and that they had their mock-sacraments of Baptism and the Supper, in some of them; their signing the
devil's book, and some shew'd the scars of the wounds
which they said were made to fetch blood with to sign the
devil's book, and some said they had imps to suck them, and
shew'd sores raw, where they said they were suck'd by them.

By these things you may see how this matter was carry'd on, viz: chiefly by the complaints and accusations of the afflicted (bewitch'd ones, as it was suppos'd) and then by the confessions of the accus'd, condemning themselves and others. Yet experience shew'd that the more there were apprehended, the more were still afflicted by Satan; and the number of confessors increasing, did but increase of the number of the accused; and the executing of some, made way for the apprehending of others: For still the afflicted complain'd of being tormented by new objects, as the former were remov'd. So that those that were concern'd, grew amaz'd at the number and quality of the persons accus'd, and feared that Satan by his wiles had enwrapped innocent persons under the imputation of that crime. And at last it was evidently seen that there must be a stop put, or the generation of the children of God would fall under that condemnation. Henceforth, therefore, the juries generally acquitted such as were tried, fearing they had gone too far before. And Sir William Phips, the Governor, repriev'd all that were condemn'd, even the confessors as well as others.

As to our case at Salem, I conceive it proceeded from some mistaken principles: as that Satan cannot assume the shape of an innocent person, and in that shape do mischief to the bodies and estates of mankind; and that the devil, when he doth harm to persons in their body or estate, it is (at least, most commonly, generally and frequently) by the help of our neighbour, some witch in covenant with the devil; and that when the party suspected looks on the parties suppos'd to be bewitch'd, and they are thereupon struck down into a fit, as if struck with a cudgel, it is a proof of such a covenant.

A Child's Example

If the children of New-England should not with an early piety set themselves to know and serve the Lord Jesus Christ, the God of their fathers, they will be condemn'd, not only by the example of pious children in other parts of the world, the publish'd and printed accounts whereof have been brought over hither, but there have been exemplary children in the midst of New-England itself, that will rise up against them for their condemnation. It would be a very profitable thing to our children, and highly acceptable to all the Godly parents of the children, if, in imitation of the excellent Janoway's "Token for Children," there were made a true collection of notable things, exemplified in the lives and deaths of many amongst us whose childhood have been signaliz'd for what is vertuous and laudable.

Mr. Thomas Thornton, the aged and faithful pastor of Yarmouth, was blessed with a daughter, nam'd Priscilla, which, at the age of eleven, left this world, having first given demonstrations of an exemplary piety.

She was one remarkably grave, devout, serious; very inquisitive about the matters of eternity; and in her partic-ular calling very diligent. She was nevertheless troubled with sore temptations and exercised about the state of her own soul; the anguish of her spirit, about her "body of death," caus'd her to pour out many tears and prayers; and she press'd that some other pious children of her acquaint-ance might with her keep a day of humiliation together, "that" (as she expressed it) "they might get power against their sinful natures." But it pleased God at length to bless the words of her godly mother for the quieting of her mind. It was her singular happiness that she had such godly parents; but it was her opinion and expression, "We trust too much to the prayers of our parents, whereas we should pray for our selves."

At last she fell mortally sick. In the beginning of her sickness, she was afraid of dying: "For," said she, "I know of no promise to encourage me." She could not but own that she had in some measure walked with God; yet she complained "that she had not found God meeting her in her prayers, and making her heart willing to be at his dispose;" and that the pride of her heart now lay as a load upon it. She own'd that she had many thoughts of Jesus

Christ, and that "it grieved her that she had sinned against him, who had done and dy'd for her."

But many days were not past before she could profess her self willing to die, with some assurance of her then going to eternal blessedness. Many thanks and loves did she now render to one of her superiours, declaring, "Twas because they had curb'd her and restrained her from sinful vanities:" And she said, "Were I now to choose my company, it should be among the people of God; I see plainly that they are the only company." She was not without her conflicts in this time, wherein one of her speeches was, "Damnation, that is the worst thing of all, but Christ is, of all, the best. I find it so: Christ is to me widsom, righteousness, sanctification and redemption." She told her father, she knew she was made up of all manner of sin; but, said she, "I hope God has humbled me, and pardon'd me in the merits of the Lord Jesus Christ." Unto her affectionate mother she said, "Mother, why do you weep, when I am well in my soul? Well, will you mourn when I am so full of joy? I pray rejoice with me."

When she was extreamly spent, she said unto her parent, "O, my father! I have been much troubled by Satan, but I find Christ is too hard for him, and sin, and all." She now said, "I know that I shall die." And being ask'd whether she were afraid of death, with a sweet smile she replied, "No, not I: Christ is better than life!" And so she continu'd in a most joyful frame, till she died; a little before which, it being the Lord's day, she ask'd what time of the day 'twas, and when they told her 'twas three of the clock, she replied, "What? is the Sabbath almost done? well, my eternal Sabbath is going to begin, wherein I shall enjoy all felicity, and sing hallelujahs to all eternity." And hereupon she quickly fell asleep in the Lord.

Book VII

A BOOK OF THE WARS OF THE LORD

Roger Williams

In the year 1654, a certain windmill in the Low Countries, whirling round with extraordinary violence, by reason
of a violent storm then blowing; the stone at length by its
rapid motion became so intensely hot, as to fire the mill,
from whence the flames, being dispersed by the high winds,
did set a whole town on fire. But I can tell my reader that,
about twenty years before this, there was a whole country in
America like to be. set on fire by the rapid motion of a
windmill, in the head of one particular man. Know, then,
that about the year 1630, arrived here one Mr. Roger
Williams; who being a preacher that had less light than fire
in him, hath by his own sad example, preached unto us the
danger of that evil which the apostle mentions in Rom. X.
2: "They have a zeal, but not according to knowledge."
Upon his arrival, the church of Salem invited him to assist
Mr. Skelton in the charge of their souls; but the governour
and council, fearing least not only that church would soon
come to have nothing of Salem in it, but also that the whole
political, as well as ecclesiastical constitution of the country, would suffer by employing a minister of his character,
did advise them to desist from "laying hands too suddenly
upon him." And that which increased in them the suspicion of his ill character, was partly, indeed, his refusing to
communicate with the church of Boston, because they
would not make a publick and solemn declaration of repentance for their communicating with the church of England, while they were in the realm of England; but partly

his violent urging, that the civil magistrate might not punish breaches of the first table in the laws of the ten commandments: which assertion, besides the door which it opened unto a thousand profanities, by not being duly limited, it utterly took away from the authority all capacity to prevent the land, which they had purchased on purpose for their own recess from such things; its becoming such a "sink of abominations," as would have been the reproach and ruin of Christianity in these parts of the world. The church taking the advice of their fathers in the state, on this occasion, Mr. Williams removed unto Plymouth, where he was accepted as a preacher for the two years ensuing.

But at Plymouth his turbulent and singular opinions not finding the entertainment which he expected, he desired a dismission back to Salem from them; and they, perceiving the giddy courses of separation, whereto he would abandon himself, and whereby he might endanger them, wisely humour'd what he desir'd. Coming to Salem, in the time of Mr. Skelton's illness, the church, affected with the fierceness of his talking in publick, and the starchtness of his living in private, so far forgot themselves, as to renew their invitations unto him to become their pastor; and tho' the government again renewed their advice unto the people to forbear a thing of such ill consequence, yet they rashly pursued their motion, and he quickly accepted it. It happened that soon after this, the church made suit unto the court, for a parcel of land, which lay commodious for their affairs; but the court, offended at the slight lately put upon them, delay'd their grant of what the church petitioned for; whereupon, incensed Mr. Williams enchants the church to join with him in writing letters of admonition unto all the churches whereof any of the magistrates were members, that they might admonish the magistrates of "scandalous injustice" for denying this petition. The neighbouring churches, both by petitions and messengers, took such happy pains with the church of Salem, as presently recovered that holy flock to a sense of his aberrations; which Mr.

Williams perceiving, though he had a little before bragg'd, "that of all the churches in the world, those of New-England were the purest; and of all in New-England, that whereof himself was the teacher;" yet he now, staying at home, sent unto the church of Salem, then assembled, a letter, to give them notice, "that if they would not separate, as well from the churches of New-England as of old, he would separate from them." His more considerate church not yielding to these lewd proposals, he never would come to their assemblies any more; no, nor hold any communion in any exercise of religion with any person, so much as his own wife, that went up unto their assemblies; but at the same time he kept a meeting in his own house, whereto resorted such as he had infected with his extravagancies.

These things were, indeed, very disturbant and offensive; but there were two other things in his quixotism, that made it no longer convenient for the civil authority to remain unconcerned about him. For, first, whereas the king of England had granted a royal charter unto the "governour and company" of this colony; which patent was indeed the very life of the colony; this hot-headed man publickly and furiously preached against the patent, as an "instrument of injustice," and pressed both rulers and people to be humbled for their sin in taking such a patent, and utterly throw it up; on an insignificant pretence of wrong thereby done unto the Indians, which were the natives of the country, therein given to the subjects of the English crown. Secondly, an order of the court, upon some just occasion had been made, that an "oath of fidelity" should be, though not imposed upon, yet offered unto the freemen, the better to distinguish those whose fidelity might render them capable of imployment in the government: which order this man vehemently withstood, on a pernicious pretence that it was the prerogative of our Lord Christ alone to have his office established with an oath; and that an oath being the worship of God, carnal persons, whereof he supposed there were many in the land, might not be put upon it. These crimes at last procured a sentence of banishment upon him.

Upon the sentence of the court, Mr. Williams with his party going abroad (as one says) to "seek their providences," removed into the southern parts of New-England, where he, with a few of his own sect, settled a place called Providence. There they proceeded not only unto the gathering of a thing like a church, but unto the renouncing of their infant-baptism; and at this further step of separation they stopped not, but Mr. Williams quickly told them, "that being himself misled, he had led them likewise out of the way;" he was now satisfied that there was none upon earth that could administer baptism, and so that their last baptism, as well as their first, was a nullity, for the want of a called administration; he advised them therefore to forego all, to dislike every thing, and wait for the coming of new apostles: whereupon they dissolved themselves, and became that sort of sect which we term Seekers, keeping to that one principle, "that every one should have the liberty to worship God according to the light of his own conscience;" but owning of no true churches or ordinances now in the word.

Mr. Williams, after this, was very instrumental in obtaining a charter for the government of Rhode-Island, which lay near and with his town of Providence, and was by the people sometimes chosen governour: but for the most part he led a more private life.

It was more than forty years after his exile that he lived here, and in many things acquitted himself so laudably, that many judicious persons judged him to have had the "root of the matter" in him, during the long winter of this retirement: He used many commendable endeavours to Christianize the Indians in his neighbourhood, of whose language, tempers and manners he printed a little relation with observations, wherein he spiritualizes the curiosities with two and thirty chapters, whereof he entertains his reader. There was always a good correspondence always held between him and many worthy and pious people in the colony, from whence he had been banish'd, tho' his keeping still so many of his dangerous principles kept the government, unto whose favour some of the English nobility had by letters recommended him, from taking off the sentence of his banishment.

Anne Hutchinson

The church of God had not long been in this wilderness, before the dragon cast forth several floods to devour it; but not the least of those floods was one of Antinomian and familistical heresies, with which the countrey began betimes to be infested. 'Tis noted of seducers that, like their father the devil, the old, the first seducer, they usually have a special design upon the weaker sex, who are more easily gained themselves, and then are fit instruments for the gaining of their husbands unto such errors as will cause them to lose their souls at last. Whereas the prime seducer of the whole faction which now began to threaten the country with something like a Munster tragedy, was a woman, a gentlewoman, of "an haughty carriage, busie spirit, competent wit, and a voluble tongue;" among whose relations at this day there are so many worthy and useful persons, that for their sakes I would gladly contrive some way to relate so important a story as that of her affairs, without mentioning of her name.

This our erroneous gentlewoman, at her coming out of Lincolnshire in England unto New-England, upon pretence of religion, was well respected among the professors of this religion; and this the more, because at the meetings of the women, which used to be called gossippings, it was her manner to carry on very pious discourses, and so put the neighbourhood upon examining their spiritual estates, by telling them how far a person might go in "trouble of mind;" and being restrained from very many evils, and constrained unto very many duties, by none but a legal work upon their souls, without ever coming to a "saving union with the Lord Jesus Christ," that many of them were convinced of a very great defect in the settlement of their everlasting peace, and acquainted more with the "Spirit of the gospel," than ever they were before. At length, under the pretence of that warrant, "that the elder women are to teach the younger," she set up weekly meetings at her house, whereto threescore or fourscore people would resort, that they might hear the sermons of Mr. Cotton repeated, but in such a sort, that after the repetition, she would make her explicatory and applicatory declamations, wherein what she confirmed of the sermons must be canonical, but what she omitted all *Apocrypha.*

It was not long before 'twas found that most of the errors, then crawling like vipers about the countrey, were hatched at these meetings; where this notable woman, who called herself another Priscilla, to "instruct others more perfectly," did set herself "most perfectly to confound" all the interests of Christianity with damnable doctrines, which maintained "our personal union with the Spirit of God," and, "the insignificancy of sanctification to be any evidence of our good estate;" and, "the pertinency of commands to work out our own salvation with fear and trembling, and give all diligence to make our calling and election sure, unto none but such as were in a covenant of works;" and, "the setting up of immediate revelation about future events, to be believed as equally infallible with the Scriptures:" and it was wonderful to see with what a speedy and spreading fascination these doctrines did bewitch the minds of people, which one would not have imagined capable of being so besotted.

She was all this while so cunning, that Mr. Cotton could get no better evidences of her broaching these opinions, than she had of her own justification; but still unto him, and such as came from him, she would express herself with a satisfying orthodoxy; however, whilst Mr. Cotton's candour was thus abused, he faithfully told her that he doubted that she would at last be found not right; and this for three things which he had observed in her: one was that her faith was not produced, and scarce ever strengthened, according to her own relation, by the public ministry of the word, but by her own private meditations and revelations; another was that she clearly discerned her justification, according to her own confession, but little or nothing at all her sanctification: A third was, that she was more sharply censorious about the states and hearts of other people, than the "self judging servants of God" used to be. And now attend the issue!

At last full proof was obtained that this gentlewoman was not the Priscilla pretended, but rather deserving the name of the prophetess in the church of Thyatira; it was proved that more than a score of Antinomian and familistical errors had been held forth by her, and the church was resolved that she should no more seduce the servants of the Lord. The admonitions of the church were by the elders, according to the rule of the gospel, given unto her; and after many endeavours of Mr. Cotton to convince her, she did seem to be convinced of her many erroneous ways, both in judgment and practice; therewithal presenting under her own hand, before the whole church of Boston — yea, before many churches then assembled at the lecture in Boston — a recantation of them. Nevertheless, under such an infatuation of pride she was, that whilst the church was debating about this recantation, she did with a strange confidence and impudence assert, "that she never was really of any opinion contrary to the declaration she had now made." However, some of her expressions had been miscon-strued: whereupon many witnesses arose, which demon-strated her guilty of gross lying in that assertion: and that caused Mr. Cotton to say, that her case was now altered: for being now convicted of lying, he thought she was to be cast out with them that "love and make a lie." So, with the full consent of the church, the sentence of excommunication was passed upon her.

But the seditions raised in the country by the means of this Virago, procured the animadversions of the court, as well as the church upon her; before which being brought, she made a canting harrangue about her "immediate reve-lations;" concluding her speech with these words:

"I will give you one place more which the Lord brought to me by immediate revelations: and that doth concern you all; it is in Dan. vi.: 'When the presidents and princes could find nothing against him, because he was faithful, they sought matter against him concerning the law of his God, to cast him into the lion's den.' So it was revealed unto me, that they should plot against me; but the Lord bid me not fear, for he that delivered Daniel and the three children, his hand was not shortned. And see this Scripture this day fulfilled in mine eyes; therefore take heed what you go about to do unto me; for you have no power over my body, neither can you do me any harm; for I am in the hands of the Eternal Jehovah my Saviour; I am at his appointment; the bounds of my habitation are cast in heaven; I fear none but the great Jehovah, who hath foretold me of these things; and I do verily believe that he will deliver me, and this by miracle, out of your hands. Therefore take heed how you proceed against me; for I know that, for this you go about to do to me, God will ruin you, and your posterity, and this whole state."

She also insisted much upon that Scripture, "Tho' I make a full end of all nations, yet will I not make a full end of thee." But the court put an end to her vapouring talk; and finding no hope of reclaiming her from her scandalous, dangerous and enchanting extravagancies, ordered her to depart out of the colony: so she went first into Rhode Island; but not liking to stay there, she removed her family unto a Dutch plantation called Hebgate; where, within a little while, the Indians treacherously and barbarously murthered them, to the number of sixteen persons, on the occasion of a quarrel they had with the Dutch thereabouts; and made an end of scarce any but her family among all the neighbour nations.

The Quakers

If the churches of our Lord Jesus Christ must in every age be assaulted by hereticks, acting under the energy of that old serpent, who knowing that as the first creation, so the new creation begins with light, hath used thousands of blinds to keep a saving light from entring into the souls of men, that being a "people of wrong understanding, he that made them shall not have mercy on them;" it must be expected that the churches of New-England should under-go some assaults from the worst of hereticks that this age has produced. Now, I know not whether the sect which hath appeared in our days under the name of Quakers, be not upon many accounts the worst of hereticks; for in Quakerism, which has by some been called, the "sink of all heresies," we see the vomit cast out in the by-past ages, by whose kennels of seducers, lick'd up again for a new diges-tion, and once more exposed for the poisoning of mankind; though it pretends unto light, yet by the means of that very pretence it leaves the bewildred souls of men "in chains unto darkness," and gives them up to the conduct of an *Ignis Fatuus:* but this I know, they have been the most venomous of all to the churches of America. The beginning of this upstart sect has been declared, by one who was a pillar of it, in a pamphlet written in the year 1659, where this passage occurs: "It is now about seven years since the Lord raised us up:" And the north of England was reckon'd the place of its nativity. Nevertheless, I can tell the world that the first Quakers that ever were in the world, were certain fanaticks here in our town of Salem, who held forth almost all the fancies and whimsies which a few years after were broached by them that were so called in England, with whom yet none of ours had the least communication.

Our Salem Quakers indeed of themselves died childless; but the numbers of those in England increasing, they did in the year 1657 find a way into New-England, where they first infested Plymouth colony, and were for a while most un-happily successful in seducing the people not only to attend unto the mystical dispensations of the light within, as having the whole of religion contained therein, but also to oppose the good order, both civil and sacred, erected in the colony. Those persons in the Massachusets-colony, whose office it was to be watchmen of it, were much alarmed at the approach of so great a plague, and were at some loss how to prevent it, and avoid it. Although Quakerism has, by the new-turn that such ingenious men as Mr. Penn have given to it, become quite a new thing; yet the old Foxian Quakerism, which then visited New-England, was the grossest collection of blasphemies and confusions that ever was heard of. They stiled those "blind beasts and liars, who should say that the Scriptures reveal God;" and affirmed it, "the greatest error in the world, and the ground of all errors, to say, the Scriptures are a rule for Christians." They said, "that the Scripture does not tell people of a Trinity, nor three persons in God, but that those three persons are brought in by the Pope." They held, "that justification by that righteousness, which Christ fulfilled in his own person without us, is a doctrine of devils." They said, "that they that believe in Christ are not miserable sinners, nor do those things they ought not to do." They said, "if the bodies of men rise again, then there is a pre-eminence in the bodies of men above the bodies of beasts, which is to give Solomon the lie." They said, "they are like to be deceived, who are expecting that Christ's second coming will be personal." They said, "those things called ordinances — as baptism, bread and wine — rose from the Pope's invention." They said, "as for that called the Lord's day, people do not understand what they say; every day is the Lord's day." And for prayer it self, they said, "all must cease from their own words, and from their own time, and learn to be silent, until the Spirit give them utterance."

The zeal of the Massachuset-colony, to preserve themselves from the annoyances of such a blasphemous and confused generation of men, caused them to make sharp laws against them, in hopes that the terror thereby given to these evil doers would keep them from any invasion upon the colony. But "they must needs go whom the devil drives;" these devil-driven creatures did but the more furiously push themselves upon the government, for the sharp which had been turned upon them; whereupon the government unhappily proceeded unto the execution of the laws in scourging, and then banishing, and (upon their mad return) executing three or four of the chief offenders: but they considered these wretches, *Non qua errones, sed qua Turbones,*[42] in thus proceeding against them. If the reader enquire with what spirit they died, I must sincerely say that, as far as I can learn, they show'd little enough of the spirit of martyrdom. They died not like the true martyrs of Jesus Christ, with the "glorious spirit of God resting" on them. A fierce, a raging, a sullen, and a revengeful spirit, and a degree of madness rather inspired them.

A great clamour hath been raised against New-England for their "persecution of the Quakers;" and if any man will appear in the vindication of it, let him do as he please; for my part, I will not. I am verily perswaded these miserable Quakers would in a little while (as we have now seen) have come to nothing, if the civil magistrate had not inflicted any civil penalty upon them; nor do I look upon haereticide as an evangelical way for the extinguishing of heresies. 'Tis true, these Quakers did manifest an intolerable contempt of authority, and needlessly pull upon themselves a vengeance, from which the authority would gladly have released them, if they would have accepted of a release; but it is also true, that they were madmen — a sort of lunaticks, daemoniacks and energumens. A Bethlehem seems to have been fitter for them than a gallows.

Indian Troubles

Two colonies of churches being brought forth, and a third conceived within the bounds of New-England, by the year 1636, it was time for the devil to take the alarum, and make some attempt in opposition to the possession which the Lord Jesus Christ was going to have of these "utmost parts of the earth." These parts were then covered with nations of barbarous Indians and infidels, in whom the "prince of the power of the air" did "work in a spirit;" nor could it be expected that nations of wretches, whose whole religion was the most explicit sort of devil-worship, should not be acted by the devil to engage in some early and bloody action, for the extinction of a plantation so contrary to his interests, as that of New-England was.

In the year 1662, Alexander, the son and heir of old Massasoit, not being such a friend to the English as his father had been before him, solicited the Narragansets to join with him in a rebellion; upon the good proof whereof, the government of Plymouth sent that valiant and excellent commander, Major General Winslow, to fetch him down before them. The major general used such expedition and resolution in this affair, that, assisted with no more than ten men, he seized upon Alexander at an hunting-house, notwithstanding his numerous attendants about him; and when the raging sachim saw a pistol at his breast, with a threatning of death to him if he did not quietly yield himself up to go down unto Plymouth with him, he yielded, though, it may be, not very quietly thereunto. Alexander was thereupon treated with no other than that humanity and civility which was always essential to the major general; nevertheless, the inward fury of his own guilty and haughty mind threw him into such a fever as cost him his life. His brother Philip succeeded him in the sagamoreship, who, after he had solemnly renewed his "covenant of peace" with the English, most perfidiously broke it by making an attempt of war upon them in the year 1671, wherein being seasonably and effectually defeated, he humbly confessed his breach of covenant, and subscribed articles of submission, whereof one was, "That in case any future difference did arise between him and the English, he would repair to the government there to rectifie matters, before he engaged in any hostile attempts."

In the year 1674, one John Sausaman, an Indian that had been sent forth from the English to preach the gospel unto his countrey-men, addressed the Governour of Plymouth with information that Philip, with several nations of the Indians besides his own, were plotting the destruction of the English throughout the country. Philip, conscious to his own guilt, pusht on the execution of his plot as fast as he could; he armed his men, and sent away their women, and entertained many strange Indians that flock'd in unto him from several parts of the country, and began to be tumultuous. The English, whose innocency and integrity had made them too secure, nevertheless, on these alarums, made several friendly applications unto Philip, with their advice that he would no more allow of any thing that should look like tumult among his people; but they were entertained with a surly, haughty, and provoking insolence. The Indians proceeded in the month of June unto the rifling of several houses in the plantations near Mount-Hope, which was the seat where Philip was kennell'd with the rest of these horrid salvages; and hereupon the Governour of Plymouth sent forth a small army for the defence of the exposed plantations.

Plymouth-colony being thus involved in a war, immediately sent unto the other United Colonies for their aid, who, according to the articles of the Union whereinto they were confederated, immediately approved themselves true brethren to the colony in adversity. The English little army scowred the woods, and with some loss to ourselves, we now and then had opportunity to inflict a greater loss upon the enemy. But we took this opportunity to march over into the Narraganset-country, that with a sword in our hands we might renew and confirm our peace with a most considerable nation of the Indians there, of whose conjunction with Philip and his Wampanoogs (for so were Philip's nation called) we had more than ordinary cause to be afraid. The effect of which was, that the sachims of the Narragansets did, on July 15, sign and seal articles of peace with us, wherein they engaged that they would not only forbear all acts of hostility against the English, but also use their utmost ability, by all acts of hostility, to destroy Philip and his adherents, calling the God of heaven to witness for the true performance of these articles.

Heaven saw more blood must be drawn from the colonies, before health could be restored to them: Philip would have surrendered himself, if we had gone in to take him; whereas, now becoming desperate, he with his best fighting men taking the advantage of a low tide in the middle of the night, wafted themselves over on small rafts of timber, into the woods that led unto the Nipmuck-country, while our forces that lay encamped on the other side perceived it not. An hundred of the miserable salvages that were left behind made a surrender of themselves to our mercy; but Philip's escape now soon after day-light being discovered, the English, assisted with a party of Monhegin-Indians, pursued them as fast as they could, and in the pursuit slew about thirty of them ere the night obliged them to give over. However, Philip now escaping to the westward, he enflamed the several nations of the Indians in the West wherever he came, to take part with him, until the flame of war was raging all over the whole Massachuset-colony.

And now behold, reader, a comfortable matter in the midst of so many tragedies! The General Court, then sitting at Boston, appointed a committee, who, with the assistance of the ministers in the neighbourhood, might suggest what were the "provoking evils" that had just brought the judgments of God in a bloody war upon the land and what laws might be enacted for the reformation of those "provoking evils!" — the return of which committee to the General Court was kindly received on October 19, and care taken further to prosecute the intentions of it. Now as our martyrologist, Mr. Fox, observes, that at the very day and hour when the act of reformation, in the reign of King Edward VI, was put in execution at London, God gave the nation a signal victory at Muscleborough: thus it was remark'd by some devout men, that on the very day when the vote was passed at Boston for the reformation of miscarriages in the land, our forces had a notable success an hundred miles off against the common enemy. Seven or eight hundred Indians broke in upon Hatfield at all quarters, but our forces being beyond their expectation lodged in the neighbourhood, the Indians were so terribly defeated, that after

the killing of but one Englishman in the fight, they confessed the "town too hot" for them, and fled so fast, that
many of them lost their lives in the river. This resolute
repulse gave such a check to the enemy, that the western
plantations for a long while heard little or nothing further
from them; some straggling parties, indeed, were here and
there mischievous; but as winter drew on, they generally
retired unto the Narraganset-country, where the reader
must now expect a considerable action! 'Tis true, the European campaigns, for the numbers of men appearing in
them, compared with the little numbers that appear in
these American actions, may tempt the reader to make a
very diminutive business of our whole Indian-war: but we
who felt ourselves assaulted by unknown numbers of devils
in flesh on every side of us, and knew that our minute
numbers employ'd in the service against them, were proportionably more to us than mighty legions are to nations
that have existed as many centuries as our colonies have
years in the world, can scarce forbear taking the colours in
the Sixth Book of Milton to describe our story: and speaking of our Indians in as high terms as Virgil of his *pismires:
It nigrum campis agmen!*43

The time limited by Heaven for the success of the Indian
treacheries was now almost expired: the blasphemy, and
insolence, and prodigious barbarity of the salvages, was
come to a sufficient heighth, for the "Lord God of Za-
baoth" to interpose his own revenges: and the impossibility
which there appeared for our people to attend their husbandry in the fields, or to find out their enemy in the
woods, did, as the spring advanced, throw us into an extremity of despair, to wade through another summer like the
last. But now was the time for deliverance! There was an
evil spirit of dissention strangely sent among the Indians,
which disposed them to separate from one another: the
demons, who visibly exhibited themselves among them at
their powawing, or conjuring, signified still unto them that
they could now "do no more for them;" the Maqua's, a

powerful nation in the west, made a descent upon them, ranging and raging through the desert with irresistible fury; fevers and fluxes became epidemical among them; and their being driven from their planting and fishing places, drove them into so much of a famine, as brought mortal sickness upon them: finally, a "visible smile of Heaven" was upon almost all the enterprizes of the English against them: and an unaccountable terror at the same time so dispirited them, that they were like men under a fascination. Thus the conquest of the Indians went on at such a rate, that whereas, June 29, 1675, was the first fast publickly observed in this colony on the occasion of the Indian troubles, now, June 29, 1676, was appointed a day of thanksgiving through the colony for the comfortable steps and hopes that we saw towards the end of those troubles.

But now, reader, prepare to make a just reflection upon that antient and famous passage of sacred Scripture, "Wo to thee that spoilest, and thou wast not spoiled! and dealest treacherously, and they dealt not treacherously with thee! when thou shalt cease to spoil, thou shalt be spoiled; and when thou shalt make an end to deal treacherously, they shall deal treacherously with thee!" One thing which emboldned King Philip in all his outrages, was an assurance which his magicians (consulting their oracles) gave him, that no "Englishman should ever kill him;" and, indeed, if any Englishman might have had the honour of killing him, he must have had a good measure of grace to have repressed the "vanity of mind" whereto he would have had some temptations. But this will not extend the life of that bloody and crafty wretch above "half his days!" A man belonging to Philip himself, being disgusted at him for killing an Indian who had propounded an expedient of peace with the English, ran away from him to Rhode-Island, where Captain Church was then recruiting of his weary forces; and upon the intelligence hereof, Captain Church, with a few hands of both English and Indians, immediately set forth upon a new expedition. That very night Philip (like the man in the army of Midian) had been dreaming that he was "faln into the hands of the English;" and now, just as he was telling his dream, with advice unto his friends to fly for their lives, lest the knave who had newly gone from them should shew the English how to come at them, Captain Church, with his company, fell in upon them; Philip attempted a flight out of the swamp, at which instant both an Englishman and an Indian endeavouring to fire at him, the Englishman's piece would not go off, but the Indian's presently shot him through his venomous and murderous heart; and in that very place where he first contrived and commenced his mischief, this Agag was now cut into quarters, which were then hanged up, while his head was carried in triumph to Plymouth, where it arrived on the very day that the church there was keeping a solemn thanksgiving to God.

Reader, 'twas not unto a Delphos, but unto a Shiloh, that the planters of New-England have been making their progress, and King Philip is not the only Python that has been giving them obstruction in their passage and progress thereunto. But if *Infaelix Exitus Persecutorum*[44] is any note of the true church, I am sure New-England has a true church to people it; for all the serpents, yea, or giants, that formerly molested that religious plantation, found themselves engaged in a fatal enterprize. We have by a true and plain history secured the story of our successes against all the Ogs in this woody country from falling under the disguises of mythology; but it administers to us the reflection which has been often made, that as of old the ruins that still overtook the persecutors of the poor Picardines caused men to say, "If a man be weary of his life, let him become an enemy to the Picardines!" The like ruins have overwhelmed them that have persecuted the poor New-Englanders. And we will not conceal the name of the God our Saviour, as an heathen country sometimes would, *Ne ab hostibus evocatus, alio Commigraret.*[45] No, 'tis our Lord Jesus Christ, worshipped according to the rules of his

NOTES

n-born inhabitants of European extraction, particularly
dian colonials.

rth those pious heroes to withstand / The sea's rough rage
gher toil on land. (Virgil's *Aeneid,* 1, 9 [altered]).

he many favors with which your bounty has enriched me, I
p one in everlasting remembrance — I mean the lesson I
ned through your Reply to the Poissy Conference, that of
n centuries since Christ, the first was the truly golden era
hurch, and that the rest have been successive periods of
y; when therefore I had the power of choosing between
eferred the golden age.

ogy.

Time's witness, the messenger of Antiquity, the lamp of
e embodied soul of Memory, the guide of human Life.
e Oratore, 11, 9 [slightly transposed]).

be admired than imitated.

le, faithful, and accurate writer.

n honey.

historian, if ever one existed.

have outdone all other Greek and Latin authors.

ne (so far as historians are concerned) the Roman
d a genius worthy of their matching empire.

acked cities, kings in flight or chains.

uld exercise leniency towards historians, and bear in
ey cannot be infallible in everything.

e narration of great transactions, with awards of praise
the actors.

be the highest office of History to blazon abroad the
race, and to hold up before depravity, whether it be
eed, the dread of eternal obloquy. (Tacitus, *Annals,*

to Diety himself when dishonour is cast on such as
in the loftiness of their virtue, or when praise is
eir opposites.

tyle of writing.

blessed gospel, who is the great Phoebus, that "Sun of righteousness," who hath so saved his churches from the designs of the "generations of the dragon."

Things to Come

From relating of things past, it would no doubt be very acceptable to the reader if we could pass to foretelling of things to come. Our curiosity in this point may easily come to a degree culpable and criminal. We must be humbly content with what the God in whose hands are our times hath revealed unto us. Two things we will venture to insert:

First, for our selves at home, let us remember an awful saying of our Goodwin, quoted by my reverend friend Mr. Noyes, in his late excellent sermon at our anniversary election: "As you look for storms in autumn, and frosts in winter, so expect judgments where the gospel hath been preached; for the quarrel of the covenant must be avenged."

Secondly, for the church abroad, I am far from deserting what was asserted in the sermon preached at our anniversary election in the year 1696:

"The tidings which I bring unto you are, that there is a revolution and a reformation at the very door, which will be vastly more wonderful than any of the deliverances yet seen by the church of God from the beginning of the world. I do not say that the next year will bring on this happy period; but this I do say, the bigger part of this assembly may, in the course of nature, live to see it. These things will come on with horrible commotions, and concussions, and confusions: The mighty angels of the Lord Jesus Christ will make their descent, and set the world a trembling at the approaches of their almighty Lord; they will shake nations, and shake churches, and shake mighty kingdoms, and shake once more, not earth only, but heaven also."

But, oh my dear New-England, give one of thy friends leave to utter the fears of thy best friends concerning thee; and consider what fearful cause there may be for thee to expect sad things to come! If every wiseman be a prophet, there are some yet in thee that can prophesie. Predictions may be form'd out of these.

Where schools are not vigorously and honourably encouraged, whole colonies will sink apace into a degenerate and contemptible condition, and at last become horribly barbarous: and the first instance of their barbarity will be, that they will be undone for want of men, but not see and own what it was that undid them.

Where faithful ministers are cheated and grieved by the sacriledge of people that rebel against the express word of Christ, "let him that is taught in the word, communicate unto him that teacheth in all good things," the righteous judgments of God will impoverish that people; the gospel will be made lamentably unsuccessful unto the souls of such a people; the ministers will either be fetch'd away to heaven, or have their ministry made woefully insipid by their incumbrances on earth.

Where the pastors of churches in a vicinity despise or neglect formed associations for mutual assistance in their evangelical services, "wo to him that is alone." 'Tis a sign either that some of the pastors want love to one another, or that others may be conscious to some fault, which may dispose them to avoid inspection; but fatal to the churches will be the tendency of either.

Where a mighty body of people in a country are violently set upon running down the ancient church state in that country, and are violent for the hedge about the communion at the Lord's table to be broken down; and for those who are not admitted unto the communion, to stand on equal terms in all votes with them that are; the churches there are not far from a tremendous convulsion, and they had need use a marvellous temper of resolution with circumspection to keep it off.

Where churches are "bent upon backsliding," and carried away with a strong spirit of apostasie, whatever minister shall set himself to withstand their evil bents, will pull

upon himself an inexpressible co[...]
merits never so great, a thousan[...]
make him little; he had need be[...]
great prayer; but God will at l[...]
with wonderful recompences.

Reader, I call these things pr[...]
all this while writing history.

Now, if any discerning perso[...]
impend over New-England, [...]
mentioned, it is to be hoped [...]
thoughts how to anticipate th[...]
the sense of all men, who di[...]
vain to hope for any good, [...]
poured out from Heaven t[...]
them to consider, whether [...]
"spirit of grace" be not hu[...]
fasting before the God of he[...]

It was therefore an article [...]
the principal ministers in [...]
mention of that advice, [...]
sleeping will follow,) I'll c[...]

"Solemn days of prayer [...]
churches, to implore th[...]
generation, would probal[...]
the turning of our you[...]
fathers. The more there [...]
more the grace of God [...]
there is in this way a n[...]
awaken our unconvert[...]
everlasting interests; wh[...]
a remarkable reformati[...]

1. Americ[...]
   West In[...]
2. Drove f[...]
   and rou[...]
3. Among [...]
   shall ke[...]
   have lea[...]
   the fiftee[...]
   of the C[...]
   degenera[...]
   them, I p[...]
4. An antho[...]
5. History is[...]
   Truth, th[...]
   (Cicero, *D*[...]
6. Rather to [...]
7. An agreea[...]
8. Sweeter tha[...]
9. A sagacious[...]
10. Appears to [...]
11. In him al[...]
    people foun[...]
12. Great wars, [...]
13. Readers sho[...]
    mind that th[...]
14. History is th[...]
    or censure to [...]
15. I deem it to [...]
    virtues of the[...]
    in word or d[...]
    111, 65).
16. It is offensiv[...]
    resemble Hi[...]
    bestowed on t[...]
17. The simplest s[...]

18. Memoirs of ecclesiastical transactions.

19. As a little salt seasons food, and increases its relish, so a spice of antiquity heightens the charm of style.

20. Ask pardon for this self-praise.

21. Every writer forms mistaken judgments of his own productions.

22. In the course of a long work.

23. Utterly incredible.

24. I first, with canvas to the gale unfurl'd, / Made the wide circuit of the mighty world.

25. A call to leave their country and their home.

26. Nile.

27. After the Massachusetts model.

28. A man in authority is a target, at which Satan and the world launch all their darts.

29. We are all the worse for it.

30. Hopes of greater and better things.

31. None can tell where fate will bear me.

32. Mother of Art, i.e., native genius. Straitened circumstances.

33. In the spirit of the Lord.

34. Execrable gowns.

35. Chastens the manners and the soul refines.

36. Our forefathers called academies by the significant name of Universities, because in them are revealed, like a hidden treasure, the universal stores of knowledge, both in divine and human things.

37. Whether it is more expedient to shut up the student at home and in his own closet, or to send him to the crowded school and to public teachers.

38. City of Books.

39. Money-lover.

40. Who seven long years has spent in student-toil.

41. My country and my sire.

42. Not as errorists, but as destroyers.

43. Forth o'er the field the tawny squadrons march.

44. Fearful is the end of persecutors.

45. Lest he should be over-persuaded, by the adulations and offerings of the foe, to desert them.

SELECTED BIBLIOGRAPHY

PRIMARY SOURCES

MATHER, COTTON. *Magnalia Christi Americana; or, The Ecclesiastical History of New-England; from its First Planting, in the Year 1620, unto the Year of Our Lord 1698.* Introduction and occasional notes by the Rev. Thomas Robbins. 2 vols. New York: Russell and Russell, 1967. Reproduced from the 1852 edition.

MURDOCK, KENNETH B., ed. *Selections from Cotton Mather.* New York: Harcourt, Brace and Co., 1926.*

FORD, WORTHINGTON C., ed. *Diary of Cotton Mather: 1681–1724.* 2 vols. Boston: Massachusetts Historical Society, 1911, 1912.

SECONDARY SOURCES

GAY, PETER. *A Loss of Mastery: Puritan Historians in Colonial America.* Berkeley and Los Angeles: University of California Press, 1966.*

MILLER, PERRY. *The New England Mind: From Colony to Province.* Cambridge, Mass.: Harvard University Press, 1953.*

MILLER, PERRY. *The New England Mind: The Seventeenth Century.* Cambridge, Mass.: Harvard University Press, 1939.*

MORISON, SAMUEL ELIOT. *The Puritan Pronaos.* New York: New York University Press, 1936.*

MURDOCK, KENNETH B. *Literature and Theology in Colonial New England.* Cambridge, Mass.: Harvard University Press, 1949.*

WENDELL, BARRETT. *Cotton Mather: The Puritan Priest.* New York: Dodd, Mead and Co., 1891.*

Currently available in a paperback edition.